COWLEY PUBLICATIONS is a ministry of the brothers of the Society of Saint John the Evangelist, a monastic order in the Episcopal Church. Our mission is to provide books and resources for those seeking spiritual and theological formation. COWLEY PUBLICATIONS is committed to developing a new generation of writers and teachers who will encourage people to think and pray in new ways about spirituality, reconciliation, and the future.

This Far by Grace

Can a church leader whose faith is centered in Christ, who loves the Bible, and who works for church unity affirm gay and lesbian relationships? Those who wonder should read this fine volume. J. Neil Alexander writes with clarity and honesty.

—HERBERT W. CHILSTROM, FORMER PRESIDING BISHOP, EVANGELICAL LUTHERAN CHURCH IN AMERICA

In This Far by Grace, *Bishop Neil Alexander offers an honest account of how his thinking has changed with regard to the complex issues of human sexuality, and especially homosexuality. Weaving solid biblical scholarship and authentic Anglican theology into his reflection, Neil shares the fruit of his own journey in a way that graciously invites the reader to do the same. This is good food for the journey.*

—THE RIGHT REVEREND THOMAS C. ELY, EPISCOPAL BISHOP OF VERMONT

A brave and honest account—at once learned and pastoral—of this bishop's struggles with the pastoral and theological issues of homosexuality and Christianity. Reading it I learned much and was often deeply moved.

—THE REV. CHARLES HACKETT, DIRECTOR, ANGLICAN STUDIES, CANDLER SCHOOL OF THEOLOGY, EMORY UNIVERSITY

This Far by Grace

*A Bishop's Journey
Through Questions
about Homosexuality*

J. Neil Alexander

A COWLEY PUBLICATIONS BOOK

Lanham, Chicago, New York, Toronto, and Plymouth, UK

Published in the United States of America by Cowley Publications, a division of the Society of Saint John the Evangelist. No portion of this book may be reproduced, stored in or introduced into a retrieval system, or transmitted, in any form or by any means—including photocopying—without the prior written permission of Cowley Publications, except in the case of brief quotations embedded in critical articles and reviews.

Library of Congress Cataloging-in-Publication Data:
Alexander, J. Neil, 1954-
  This far by grace : a bishop's journey through questions about homosexuality / J. Neil Alexander.
      p. cm.
Includes bibliographical references.
  ISBN 1-56101-224-6 (pbk. : alk. paper)
  1. Homosexuality—Religious aspects—Christianity. I. Title.
BR115.H6A44 2003
261.8'35766—dc22

                                        2003022309

Unless otherwise noted, Scripture quotations are taken from *The New Revised Standard Version of the Bible*, © 1989, by the Division of Christian Education of the National Council of the Churches of Christ in the United States of America. Used by permission.

Cover design: Jennifer Hopcroft

This book was printed in the United States of America

A Cowley Publications Book
Published by Rowman & Littlefield Publishers, Inc.
A wholly owned subsidiary of
The Rowman & Littlefield Publishing Group, Inc.
4501 Forbes Boulevard, Suite 200, Lanham, Maryland 20706
http://www.rowmanlittlefield.com

Estover Road, Plymouth PL6 7PY, United Kingdom

Distributed by National Book Network

Contents

INTRODUCTION
The Gift of Pragmatism

THIS IS THE STORY OF ONE PERSON'S journey with questions on the issue of homosexuality. It is a personal story that covers most of my life thus far. I have not written it with the intention of changing anyone's mind, nor have I tried to construct most of what follows in the form of an argument. It is not intended to be an academic treatise on the biblical and theological questions concerning homosexuality, nor is it intended to be a lengthy pastoral reflection on the questions before the church. Elements of those and other aspects of theological writing are visible in the text, but it is important that the reader receive this as my story, something akin to the diary of a pilgrimage.

All writing is autobiographical. Whether we are talking about imaginative fiction or the narrative of complicated scholarly research, the results will inevitably tell you a great deal about the author. This little book is no exception. My own motivation for writing this developed during the long days of the Seventy-fourth General Convention of the Episcopal Church, in the summer of 2003. In so many ways, it was a wonderful gathering of the church. Whether one is pleased or saddened by some of the actions of the Convention, it would be hard not to agree that the gathering was quintessentially Anglican. Everyone was at the table. Every voice was respected and honored. We prayed, we sang, we studied, we deliberated, we loved, we cried, and we did ourselves proud, as a church gathered, to engage God's mission. Although it certainly had its share of agonizing moments, from beginning to end, I was proud to be an Episcopalian.

I have struggled with the biblical and theological questions around homosexuality as a believer, as a priest and theological teacher, and, more recently, as a bishop. I have considered those questions from a variety of perspectives over a long period of time. The engagement around those important questions at the General Convention, however, required me to think through them in a way that was more demanding of me personally, spiritually, and theologically. It is one thing to study and contemplate such questions to satisfy one's own curiosity; as a teacher it is easy to hide in the underbrush of seminary lectures that present the full scope of interpretations in the interest of objectivity. It is a very different task to be a bishop and to have to decide which interpretation, which understanding of the biblical texts, or which strain of apostolic and catholic tradition will inform one's decisions, and one's votes, on important matters. It is an interesting place to be when someone says, "Bishop, I know there are fifteen possible explanations of this or that, but what I want to know is, which of those explanations is the most convincing to *you?*" Things quickly become autobiographical and self-revelatory.

So it was in the context of the General Convention that I decided I needed to write the story of my own journey with those important questions—the story up to the present time—as a discipline to help me understand the journey more fully. It has been immensely helpful to retrace the paths of my journey, and to be able to look afresh at how far I have come over the years. Putting on paper the major chapters of my story has been something like reading through old sermons, a marvelous source of spiritual autobiography for those of us who have done time in the pulpit. In those moments when I wonder if God is still present in my life, I'll read a batch of sermons from twenty years ago. It's great spiritual tonic, not because the sermons of yesteryear were any good, but because they stand as a testimony to how far I have come, and a reminder that I still have a way to go.

One way to understand the life of faith is to see it as the story of conversion, or perhaps better, as a lifelong sequence of conversions. The more one studies the Scriptures and the great theological texts of the tradition, the more such conversions one will be required to survive. The more one places one's life in the care of other Christians, the more one is likely to experience one's conversions through the eyes of others. The more time one spends actively waiting on the spirit of the risen Christ, the more one is likely to be able to see the animating presence of God active in one's life in ways that were previously invisible. The more one gives of one's time or means to the service of Christ by serving others, the more one begins to see the richness of one's own poverty. The possibility of conversion—of living ever more deeply in the risen life of Christ—is an ever-present reality. The best way to see any of this is to study how far we have come. Each of the chapters that follow is about some of the conversions I have been blessed to have experienced. I pray that there are many more to come.

The decision to prepare this material for publication came at the urging of a variety of folks. I am grateful for their encouragement. In some small way, it also represents my desire to be as transparent as possible before the church I am called to serve as a bishop. In the Anglican tradition, we got over the need to agree with one another centuries ago. One of the glories of our way of being faithful is to hold together, in creative tension, a cacophony of diverse voices, a rich continuum of temperaments, and almost as many ways of knowing as there are things to be known. It's often tense, but never boring! My daily work as a bishop places me in the midst of it all; at the same time, I must make some effort to be clear about where I am standing. My position is not about what others must think or do, or even what the church must think or do, but is, in some sense, to be a gift to others so that they can more easily find the place where they need to stand. It is not necessary that we all stand in the same place, but it is essential that we all stand together.

Perhaps just now, in the Episcopal Church and in the Anglican Communion, it is good to consider where we stand. Some years ago Harvey Guthrie, one of the great teachers and theologians of the Episcopal Church, wrote an introductory essay to a collection of articles on Anglican spirituality.[1] In his essay Guthrie noted three basic types of churches in the United States: confessional churches, experiential churches, and pragmatic churches.

Confessional churches are those that are held together by a common confession of faith beyond the Scriptures and the catholic creeds. Roman Catholics and Lutherans come to mind. These are churches with volumes of dogmatic and confessional documents that explicate the agreed-on theological positions and moral frameworks. The allegiance to such confessional documents is the principal tie that binds those churches together. In the Episcopal Church, we certainly have confessional-type documents as part of our historical heritage, but we have never subscribed to them as definitive and unchangeable statements of faith and practice.

In experiential churches, most of which originate in America, a particular sort of religious experience is the glue that holds the church together. It could be any of a multitude of possibilities: walking the sawdust trail, speaking in tongues, a unique revelatory encounter, or some other experience of the holy, shared in common. Those churches seem always to be fighting schism. Because particular experiences of God are hard to repeat, new manifestations of God's presence are often divisive. New experiences require new responses, but old experiences have become the community standard—the tie that binds—and it is hard to let go of them.

The Episcopal Church is neither of the above. We are, by contrast, a pragmatic church. We recognize the authority of Holy Scripture, and we believe that the catholic creeds are faithful summaries of apostolic faith, but we are not a confessional church, like the Roman Catholics or Lutherans, bound by a book of doctrinal decisions separate from the Scriptures, the catholic creeds, and the Book of Common Prayer. We certainly have a theological tradition, but it is not codified with the specificity that is characteristic of confessional churches. It is a characteristic of Anglicanism to encourage personal discovery, intellectual freedom, and respect for the conscience of the individual. To put it another way, we certainly have discernible theological frameworks, but we also give one another a fair amount of elbow room within them.

Nor are we an experiential church. We have all had experiences of the divine holiness, but we do not hold such experiences in common. Some of us have had classical, charismatic, Holy Ghost regeneration. Others of us are frightened by the very thought of such a thing. Some of us have received supernatural spiritual healing of body or soul, but others of us have quite different explanations of similar life transformations. Some of us have been profoundly shaped by the spiritual disciplines of the catholic tradition, but others of us are richly fed by more recent renewal movements that are gifts of the church's evangelical wing.

What, then, does it mean to be pragmatic? It means that within the generous capacity of the Episcopal Church, we do not always agree on matters of biblical interpretation or theological definition. It means that we have all gotten here by way of hundreds of different and often quite unique experiences of God's presence in our lives. It means that those things on which other churches depend to hold themselves together will never be the central feature of our common life. We find our life together driven by our willingness to stand together at the table of God's gracious hospitality. We gather in public assembly—an inherently political act— to confess that Jesus Christ is Lord. We break open the sacred texts of the tradition because we always hear them more fully when we listen together as a gathered community of faith. We stand together in all our diversity and intercede for those we love, and for those we do not even know, convinced that such common prayer really does make a difference. We tell God what God already knows about, things done and left undone, and we take the risk of doing so in one another's company. We embrace one another with words and gestures of peace, not because we always love one another but because God loves each and every one of us, all the time. We share the simple food of bread and wine, sincerely believing that it is for us the bread of heaven and the cup of salvation. We make our way back into the world, filled with the risen life of Christ, to do the best we can to be faithful servants. Every few days, and at least once a week on Sunday, we gather again at God's table, and life begins again, as if for the first time.

That, I believe, is the pragmatism at the heart of what it means to be an Episcopalian. We are a variegated tapestry of theology and experience, and we are all the richer for it. But no level of theological agreement or experiential commonality will ever be the basis on which Episcopalians will live together well. What is possible is that we will be pragmatic—we will keep our differences in perspective—and we will recognize that ultimately nothing will divide those who are willing to stand together before God's altar to sing, to pray, and to receive the gift of God's eternity.

The pragmatism of being an Episcopalian is a wonderful gift. Over the years I have lived and worked in both confessional and experiential churches. Passing through those churches has been important to my spiritual formation. Each has its own integrity; each its own goodness. But it was not until I became an Episcopalian that I began to catch on to some very important things that have been transformative in my own life in Christ. I used to believe that the important thing was what I believed about God. I have discovered that the really important thing is what God believes about me. I used to believe that the purpose of being a Christian was to learn to live a good and righteous life. I now believe that I am good and righteous, not of my own doing but as a gift of grace by faith in Jesus Christ. I used to believe that if I said my prayers and lived an obedient life, when I died I would inherit eternal life. Now I believe that eternal life begins at the font and goes on forever. My experience of God has shifted from fear to love, from conditional to unconditional, from judgment to mercy. I used to believe that being a Christian was about me. That's idolatry. I've discovered, thanks to the witness of the Episcopal Church, that being a Christian is about God. That's grace. And every last one of those conversions, and many, many more, has taken place as I have stood before the altar of God, alongside all manner of people that *God has chosen* to be my friends.

___

No book is really a solitary exercise. Over the years I have consumed thousands of pages of biblical exegesis and spent time doing theological, moral, and pastoral reflection on the subject of human sexuality in general and homosexuality in particular. I have been blessed to have hundreds of conversation partners who have taught me, argued with me, consoled me, and converted me. I am deeply grateful for everyone who has walked this way with me, whether in person or in print. There are far too many to even begin to thank them individually. Given the personal nature of this story, that is probably not appropriate anyway. This is a journey for all of us. Wherever we are along the way, none of us is ever alone. Thanks be to God!

---

[1] Harvey H. Guthrie, "Anglican Spirituality: An Ethos and Some Issues," in William J. Wolf, ed., *Anglican Spirituality* (Harrisburg, PA: Morehouse, 1982) 1–16.

A Personal Journey

THIS IS THE STORY OF A JOURNEY that spans more than thirty years. I do not remember a time when gay and lesbian persons were not a part of my life. As a youngster I did not understand what it was all about. Growing up in the South in the late fifties and early sixties, it was not something one talked about openly. It was not something one asked one's elders about.

In elementary school we developed a whole vocabulary for homosexual persons that was derogatory and demeaning. I'll spare you the details. The intent of the words was clearly to hurt and exclude. We were not very discriminating about whether the words we were hurling at each other were accurate. That wasn't the point. The point was to put someone outside the inside circle. It was about keeping certain people at a distance so they could not contaminate the purity of those of us who were perfect.

I have reflected a great deal over the years about what it meant to be perfect. I put it that way because I think we really believed it, at least at that time. After all, we were white, male, straight, and Protestant. Growing up when and where I did, it seems to me that that was the operative definition of *perfect*. We never spoke of it in those terms. We didn't have to. Even as ten-year-olds in grade school, we knew we had the upper hand by almost any measure one wanted to use. Being white and male gave us privilege; being straight and Protestant imputed a sort of populist righteousness. A sense of moral superiority was taken for granted.

Looking back on it now, it is clear that part of what was happening was a struggle for self-definition on the basis of *not* being someone else.

Being white meant that one wasn't black (or Hispanic or Asian or Jewish or Native American, to mention some of the "lesser kinds" that we had heard about but didn't actually know personally). Being white meant that we went to better schools, we lived in better neighborhoods, and our parents made better salaries. It was just better everything. Or so we believed.

Being a boy was also important. Everyone could see clearly that girls were different, and we supposed that that meant a lot of things, not all of which were bad. But by not being boys, we knew that girls were somehow not as good as they could be. They could be smarter, more socially adaptable, more versatile, more anything, but it was never enough. After all, they were girls.

In my world it was also important to be Protestant. That meant, at the least, that you didn't go to church as often (it was rumored that some of *them* went to daily mass), you didn't worship idols, and you didn't pray to Mary or those other not-god guys, only to Jesus. It didn't seem to matter that the family across the street had daily Bible study and prayer together. Because they were Catholics and we were Protestants, the kids were not allowed to play together. Something might rub off. When I was about ten, the father of some buddies down the street got caught in a fairly serious public scandal that was riddled with sexual intrigue. Even in the face of that, it was okay to play with them because they were Protestants. It took me years to sort out all that.

Those of us in the inside circle assumed that we were all straight. As it turned out, that was not true. In high school we were a united antiqueer front, but as the years passed, we realized that some of our number had disappeared. What did that mean? Only later did we discover that it was because they had finally faced the fact that they were gay. I am glad to say that the rest of us had the grace to go find them and keep them in the circle of lifelong buddies. By some mystery I'll never be able to explain, I realized that if some of my lifelong friends had come to the point of accepting themselves, I would have to come to the point of accepting them, too, even in the face of not really understanding what it was all about.

I did not grow up in a tolerant context. We were racists, if not white supremacists. We were misogynous. We were anti-Catholic. We were homophobic. Everything seemed to be based on *not being* someone else. The sad thing, looking back on it now, was that most of this was reinforced by the church. I remember, as vividly as if it were yesterday, being lined up outside the church in my junior-choir robe waiting for the service to begin, and watching the ushers turn away a black family at the door. The church's rhetoric was that "all are welcome." I could see as a youngster that it really wasn't true. The hypocrisy still hurts.

I remember, a few years later, going to Sunday school, and discovering that I had a new teacher. When I asked where our regular teacher was, I was told simply that he wouldn't be back. Sometime later I discovered that he had been removed as a teacher and sent on his way because he was gay. I remember well the righteous indignation of the pastor and some of the adults around the church. I also remember that the kids in the Sunday school class didn't understand. We missed our teacher. We liked him because he would tell us stories from the Bible rather than lecture us on being good little boys. (Sorry, the girls were in a different class. We weren't allowed to talk together about religious things in those days.)

When we graduated from the junior department of the Sunday school, we were all given Bibles of our own. I still have mine. That summer we all (just us boys, of course) went to a camp that was owned by the church. It was for indoctrination. The assumption was that we were all on the verge of growing up, that the hormones were about to start buzzing, and that we needed to get trained so we would not stray from the righteous way. We played a little softball, sang a few songs, and ate the usual camp grub, but we spent most of our time in small groups of three twelve-year-olds and an older man, going methodically through every Bible verse he could find to help us learn how to stay on the straight and narrow.

I remember well the discussion of what would come to pass us if we didn't get all that right. It took place the night before we went home, and the discussion was about God's uncontrollable anger and the eternal punishment that awaited us. At one point in the exercise, my teacher lit a match, blew it out, and touched my arm with the hot matchstick. He repeated that action with each boy in the group. He told us that if we did not live according to what he had taught us that week, then the little burn on our arms would be multiplied all over our bodies for all eternity. That was thought of as Christian education. Today I am more inclined to think of it as brainwashing, if not child abuse.

It was years before I was able to tell my parents about that experience, but somehow I think they knew that something had happened at camp to change my life forever. The next Sunday, when we pulled into the parking lot at our church, I got out of the car and walked in the opposite direction to another church a couple of blocks away. My parents watched me go without saying a word. As God's grace would have it, that Sunday the Moravian Church was having a love-feast. The opening hymn began, "Christian hearts in love united, seek alone in Jesus rest." It was wonderful to find a church that believed that God loves me *just as I am*, with or without a plea.

In high school I started going to a Bible study group led by a renegade pastor who had been thrown out of his church. I never knew the reason. About forty of us met in a garage that had been converted into a classroom. We all brought our Bibles: the thumb-indexed, red-lettered edition. After a few songs, the pastor would teach us the Bible. We would take notes and underline. We would record his wisdom as if it were directly from heaven. I learned a great deal from him. Much of what he taught me has held up well over time.

Perhaps it was because he was teaching a group of teenagers, or maybe it was because of his own personal struggles, but we talked a lot about sex and sexuality, marriage and the family, and, of course, what he called "straight talk on homosexuality." (It was years before I caught the pun.) What that meant was that he was teaching a literal reading of the English text of a handful of verses that were clearly and unambiguously against same-sex behavior. He convinced me. He went word by word through Sodom and Gomorrah, Leviticus, Romans, and all the rest, carefully arguing that there was no other way to understand the passages than the way he understood them. His arguments seemed logical, convincing, and nondebatable. My heart, my experience of gay persons in the church, and my gut told me something different, but he persuaded my mind. That was part of his argument, too. He told us that sometimes we might want to see those things differently because of feelings or some experience to the contrary, but he insisted that the mind must always be in control. I believed that, too.

In spite of my personal reservations, he had done his job quite well. I got through college, seminary, ordination, and some parish experience, completely convinced that there was only one way to read the Bible on same-sex behavior. Deep in my soul, I wondered if my thinking was too rigid, but my mind stayed in control: the Bible said same-sex behavior was wrong, and that was that. I lived with more than a little uneasiness about the fact that my seminary education helped me to be a more faithful interpreter of the Bible when it came to other subjects. It was easy to see that many passages in the Bible do not mean what they appear to mean on the surface. I was convinced that the deeper meaning of the biblical text is often buried well beneath a literal reading of the English text. I saw quickly, with the help of my professors, that all translations are imperfect, that all translations bear the theological biases of their authors, and that there is no such thing as a singular, definitive, once-and-for-all reading of the sacred texts. With all of that, I still refused to believe that the passages on same-sex behavior could mean anything other than what a literal reading of the English text said they did. This troubled me, but I couldn't get beyond it. I simply had to wait on the Lord.

After some time in parish ministry, it was my privilege to enter doctoral studies to prepare for a ministry in seminary teaching. It was a difficult transition, to say the least. I missed the vigorous community of parish life. I wondered if I was suited to the more solitary vocation of a scholar and teacher. I greatly missed the pastoral work—presiding at the Eucharist and Baptism, preaching, visiting the sick, offering spiritual counsel to the weary—and the seminary environment did not provide an adequate substitute. My wife and I were new parents, far away from our families and from the daily support of our parish. It was a hard time for our marriage.

Several weeks into graduate school, one of the senior professors could tell that I was struggling. We began to have regular conversations, rarely formally, usually on the fly, but we stayed in close contact over the next year or more. I have never been so well pastored, before or since. He was amazingly skilled at knowing when to push and when to back off. His words would sometimes sting, but always lovingly. He often referred me to passages in the Scriptures that he thought might help. Every time we talked, he inquired about the state of my prayer life.

His greatest gift was to help me establish a more faithful life of prayer. What growing up in the church, attending seminary, ordination, and parish ministry had never accomplished, this priest, by God's grace, made possible. He was God's agent in calling me to a life of prayer—sometimes gently, sometimes sternly—but he called me nonetheless. God worked mightily through this servant, who helped me to see that life and ministry were going to be stressful, if not impossible, without being grounded in a life of prayer. He never said that it would be easy. He never suggested that it would work like magic. He said that it would be as hard a work as I would ever do. But until I learned to pray—not say prayers, but pray—then all that I was experiencing, and all that lay ahead, would be more difficult than I could imagine.

Who was this man? He was an Episcopal priest, a professor of pastoral theology, a man of gentleness and grace. He was also gay. I knew him for well more than a year before I found out that he was gay. All that he had given me, he gave without me knowing, or even suspecting, that he was gay. I stumbled on that quite by accident. One evening we were having a community meeting. I have long since forgotten why the dean had called us together. I only remember that as the conversation went on, this extraordinary priest who had been used by God to change my life, stood up to speak. At first he gave eloquent testimony and spoke about what the Scriptures and the theological tradition might have to say about our discussion that evening. He then went on to say that perhaps he would also add a further perspective *as a gay man.* When those words came out of his mouth, I was spellbound. I was speechless. I froze. The meeting was soon over. I walked home alone. I didn't know what to say or think.

It wasn't like that was the first time I had ever encountered a gay person in the church. I had known plenty of them. In the parish I had been *their* pastor. But this was different. This was the first time that I was on the receiving end of *their* ministry. I was more than a little uncomfortable about having opened up my life, the struggles in my marriage, my insecurities about my new vocation, and all the rest to the *spiritual care of a gay priest.*

As the year had progressed, I had checked the chapel schedule often, and tried never to miss when he was presiding or preaching. His sermons were rich food for me in that difficult year of transition. He was too good a priest to preach just to me, but many days his sermon was so clearly on target that it seemed as though he *was* preaching directly to me. At times it was eerie. And now to discover that he was gay. It threw me for a loop.

After a few days, I finally confided in a friend that I was having real trouble with it. He didn't have much counsel, but he reached to his bookshelf and handed me two short novels by Graham Greene, *The Power and the Glory* and *Monsignor Quixote*. Each is the story of a whiskey priest whose personal life is in shambles, but whose pastoral ministrations are still valid and who is still used by God to change people's lives. I got the point, but it wasn't enough. I thought, it's one thing to be a tired, old whiskey priest struggling with a thousand temptations, but quite another to be gay. The insights gleaned from Greene's work provided a beginning, but only that.

In due course I called and made a lunch date with the gay priest who had changed my life. I think he knew what was happening in me. He was present to me with a clear sense of immediacy. He was not the least bit anxious. He was as gentle and graceful as always. I began by telling him what he had meant to me over the last year, that he might well have saved my vocation, probably saved my marriage, and certainly gave me a precious gift by teaching me how to pray. I told him about how I reacted to his public confession that he was gay. He mused that it was hardly a confession because I was probably the only person in the room who received that revelation as news. That stung.

As we talked more, he suggested that the best thing I could do to work through this was to spend more time studying the Scriptures. After all, wasn't that the problem? I had read the Scriptures, and I knew what they said. When I asked him how he "got around" the texts that prohibit same-sex behavior, he was gentle but strikingly clear: "I don't live my life, or practice my priesthood, trying to get around the Scriptures. I live my life trying to understand the sacred texts more fully and to live more deeply in the truth of them for the sake of my soul . . . and for the sake of your soul, for that matter!" With that, lunch was over, with the promise to talk more on another day.

As I walked home, I came again to the realization that this devoted priest had once more taught me something that would have life-changing consequences. When we began our lunch together, I was utterly confident that I knew exactly what the Scriptures said about same-sex behavior. I fully expected that he would be defensive and give me a multitude of reasons that the Scriptures were wrong or irrelevant. I thought he might regale me with a carefully crafted "gay theology." At the least he would suggest that my old thinking was just that, and that I should "get with the program." He did none of the above. Not even close. He was a smart enough priest to understand that if it was the Scriptures that had formed my opinions, it would have to be the Scriptures that changed them. He tried to convince me of nothing. He simply sent me back to the Scriptures, urging me to keep at it. I did, and I am grateful.

God has used more ways than I can count to get through to me at different times in my life. The Scriptures have been my companion for as long as I can remember. I have thought of the Bible as a treasure chest, with the pearl of great price—the risen Christ—its most precious jewel. I have sometimes thought of the Bible as a stunning, jeweled setting of the Hope diamond—the risen Christ—and that all the other stories, teachings, and exhortations are there to refract the light, to shine their light ever more brightly on that precious stone at the center of it all. I can't imagine life without those priceless texts.

God has also used the church to shape my life. Most of what I know about almost everything, I have learned from the church. Most of the schools I attended were schools of the church. All the schools in which I taught were schools of the church. Most of the frameworks of intelligibility through which I try to understand life are, in fact, theological frameworks I learned from the church. It might well be a sign of my own personal poverty, but thus far I possess few ways of knowing and being that are not gifts of the church, for better or for worse.

The church has also shaped me through the disciplines of liturgy and prayer, the sacraments of Christ, and the fellowship of the faithful. I can't imagine being part of a nonliturgical, nonsacramental faith community. I respect those who can be, but I am not strong enough in faith to live without those grace-filled gifts of the church. The ritual patterns of our common prayer feed my soul in ways I can only begin to explain. The richness of symbol—word, water, wine, bread, oil, space, music, movement, sound, art, color, fabric, touch—reaches deep in my soul. I am grateful for those times when I can clear away enough of the clutter of my life so that the liturgy's prayer can live in me in a fresh way, and call me deeper into the risen life of Christ. I wish such moments happened more often, but I have learned to be patient and to wait for them. Many days that's hard.

God also sneaks up on me once in a while. Funny how that works. Sometimes it is a piece of art that was not intended to have a spiritual meaning. Once in a while, I discover God speaking to me in a song or a piece of music that was not composed with religious intent. Occasionally it has been an encounter in nature, a sunset, the southern rim of the Grand Canyon early in the morning, or the multifaceted twinkle of a single star against the backdrop of a black sky. I believe that God promises to be in certain places—in word and prayer, in the sacraments of the church, in the hearts of the faithful—but God is not limited to being present with us in the old-fashioned way. God's presence can be seized all over the place if we are willing to watch and wait for it.

However, God uses another means to get through to me: other people. Of all the ways that God reaches for me, all of which I cherish, none is more fundamental than life together with fellow believers, fellow sinners redeemed, fellow servants trying to be faithful, fellow seekers of grace and forgiveness. It took me years to figure that out. I guess I am a slow learner.

I have always believed the old saying about Christianity being a relationship, but it has taken most of my life to get my mind and heart around it. When I was younger, I interpreted it to mean that being a Christian was about a personal relationship with Jesus Christ. I still believe that, but I have also come to understand that it is only part of what it means to be in relationship with God. Christian believing is also about active participation in a whole web of relationships—with God, with fellow believers, with nonbelievers, with sinners of all sorts, with folks I like and those I don't, with the whole of God's creation in all its infinite diversity. Faithful Christian believing does not offer the possibility of cutting off relationship with anyone. Sometimes we need to take a break from one another, and that can be a good thing. Sometimes we need to let emotions level off, let tempers cool, and allow a clearer perspective to come into focus. Permanent cutoffs, however, damage not only our relationships; they injure our health and our sense of wellness, and they impede any chance that we have of wholeness.

God is a relationship. That is the fundamental truth at the heart of the doctrine of the Holy Trinity. God—Father, Son, and Spirit, Creator, Redeemer, Sustainer, who was, is, and is to come—lives in dynamic relationship and models for us the relational interdependence of a holy life. It is of the very nature of God to be in relationship. Made in God's image, we, too, are designed to be in relationship with God and with one another. That is the way we are wired. That is the deep longing of every heart. It is in our DNA. To try to live otherwise is unnatural, unholy, and unacceptable—if we are to live whole, healthy, and faithful lives.

So, a big part of Christian believing is being in relationship with other people. I have been called to listen to the stories of fellow servants of Christ who are gay and lesbian. They are called to listen to my stories as well. Only when we live together, with open minds and undefended hearts, will we be able to find that gracious place beyond the present moment toward which God is calling us.

Before going on, however, an important point needs to be made here. A number of years ago, I was having a conversation with a wonderful, old curmudgeon in the parish that I was serving at the time. I think it is fair to say that he was against pretty much everything. Ask him about the town, the country, the church, the president, the bishop, whatever you wanted, and he could instantly cough up the most negative point of view imaginable. He was a stark contrast to his wife, who seemed to love everything and everybody all the time. They were a complementary pair!

One day when we were talking, we found ourselves discussing the subject of homosexuals in the church. At that time I was still rigid in my convictions on the matter, and I was not about to allow for much wiggle room in the conversation. Given my previous experience of this man, I was confident that he was going to pull out his own supply of negative clichés, and that we would find ourselves in perfect agreement. Much to my surprise, he proceeded to tell me that he had thought long and hard about homosexuals in the church. There was a distinction that he thought was important and not to be missed. I was all ears.

He believed that what upset most people in the church about homosexuals is that they thought of them as "homosexuals who were trying to act like Christians." In other words, they were homosexuals first, and Christians, a distant second, at least. "If that's the way you understand it," he said, "then it is never going to be very comfortable for you." He said that it was important to know those friends as fellow believers, as Christians first, as fellow travelers who understand their sexual orientation to be secondary. Frankly, I had never thought of it that way before. I was still in the negative column, but this faithful, old layman, who had seen pretty much everything, had dealt a severe blow to the confidence I had in my position.

As I have continued to think about this over the years, I believe he was on to something in a variety of ways. When someone asks me about who I am, the first thing I say is that I am a Christian. Then I talk about being a husband and a father. If the conversation keeps going, I talk about what I do, and what it's like to be a bishop. After that we begin to talk about siblings and extended family, friends and colleagues, and others who have been an important part of shaping my life. Then we talk about the places I've been, the schools I've attended, the things I enjoy in my spare time, and on and on. I don't remember such a conversation in which the fine points of being a heterosexual ever came up.

I once asked a friend what it was like to be a gay priest. I am lucky to still be alive. He was not amused. "*Gay*," he insisted, "is not an adjective that modifies *priest!*" He pinned my ears back in no uncertain terms about the fact that he was a priest of Christ's one, holy, catholic, and apostolic church, period. "I hope that when I die, the church will be able to put *faithful* in front of *priest* when I am buried, but other than that, my priesthood needs no special qualifiers." I knew he had me when he asked me if I had ever introduced myself as a *heterosexual priest*. I hadn't, of course. In terms of what makes me who I am, my sexual orientation is well down the list. I have discovered that it is no different for our gay and lesbian priests. "Gay priest," I have come to believe, is heterosexist terminology.

That faithful curmudgeon in my parish challenged my perspective. I am grateful. I have come a long way. I have discovered that the homosexual persons in our parishes on any given day are there because they are *baptized Christians first,* and that their sexuality, while not unimportant, is much further down the inventory of attributes that define who they understand themselves to be. They care deeply about their life of faith, they cherish the Scriptures with as much love and devotion as the rest of us, and they reach for the love and acceptance of the church because it is for them the same sort of saving lifeline that all of us hold on to for dear life.

I have also come to appreciate the fact that the majority of gay and lesbian persons who are in the church are among us because they have made a clear and unambiguous choice. We all know that there is an underground "homosexual lifestyle" that is to be abhorred, for precisely the same reasons that the underbelly of the "heterosexual lifestyle"—prostitution, pornography, pedophilia, and so on—is to be abhorred as well. It is my belief that the gay and lesbian persons in our churches are those who have said "No!" to the underworld of their sexual orientation, just as those of us who are straight have said "No!" to the underworld of sexual perversion and exploitation associated with us.

I believe that we are all *baptized Christians first and foremost.* In this sinful, painful, tragedy-ridden world, putting the gospel of Jesus at the center of one's life is a radical choice. But it is the choice that many of us—straight and gay—have made, and it is the decision that most clearly defines who we are. Everything else is secondary. That doesn't mean that it's easy. It doesn't mean that we don't lose our grip on goodness and become again the very sinners that we condemn. But it does mean that we are in relationship with a living Savior, with one another, and with the spiritual resources to make that decision the most consecrated choice in all our lives.

It has been a long, complicated, painful, and confounding journey over many years as I have struggled to open my mind, my heart, and my arms to my gay and lesbian brothers and sisters. There have been potholes, wrong turns, detours, and times of being lost and directionless. But it is a journey that I wouldn't exchange for anything in the world. Along the way, as I hope you have seen, I have encountered *texts and people.* It could not have been otherwise. This journey has been about the Bible—how to understand it more deeply and follow it more closely. It has been about those people God has put in my path along the way—some gay and lesbian, some straight, some simply conversation partners in a mutual struggle—but all of them essential to the work of God within me.

I have no reason to believe that the journey is over. I've come a long way in thirty years, but I suspect that there is more road to be traveled. God has been faithful even in times of my own blindness, weakness, and inability to be open to what God was doing in my life, in the church, and in those around me. I have every confidence that God will be faithful as I continue my journey in the future. I am this far by grace. Grace will lead me home.

The Journey with Scripture

IN THE CHURCH'S CONVERSATIONS in all matters, the Holy Scriptures of the Old and New Testament play a central role. As Episcopalians we have historically placed Scripture alongside reason and tradition as the three-pronged standard by which we understand the faith and make important decisions. This "three-legged stool" has been for many of us a useful image. It helps us to keep balance in our theological system; it helps us to keep ourselves and our church from getting sidetracked into interpretations that cannot easily be sustained.

Personally, I prefer to think of the Anglican way as more like a tricycle. I don't remember where I first ran across that idea, but it has been helpful to me over the years. The big front wheel of the tricycle is Holy Scripture. It leads the way; it is responsible for steering, for determining the overall direction in which we are going. But essential to the tricycle are its two back wheels: reason and tradition. Those back wheels bring balance and stability to the tricycle, and make the ride a great deal more reliable. I remember well what it was like to ride a tricycle as a young child, and to lose one or both of the back wheels. No matter how hard you pedaled the big front wheel, the tricycle simply made circles and ripped up the lawn. Sometimes the thing would bog down completely.

I think the image of a tricycle may be helpful to us just now. Parts of the Christian family might prefer the image of a unicycle—*sola scriptura,* Scripture alone—and they try to order their life accordingly. I respect that view and honor those who believe it is possible to follow it. But such has never been the Anglican way.

An Anglican Approach to Scripture

Anglicans have always subscribed to a high view of Scripture and scriptural authority (and let's not forget that we read more Scripture on a typical Sunday morning in the Episcopal Church than most so-called Bible churches would read in a month or more), but we have always held the Scriptures in tension with our God-given use of reason and the inheritance of the tradition of the church. (Many Anglicans, not the least of whom was John Wesley, the founder of Methodism, would add a fourth dimension, that of experience. How we *experience* the power of the Holy Spirit in our lives is for many an additional lens through which truth is to be observed.)

Through the centuries reason and tradition have been critical aspects of the faith community's method of interpreting the Scriptures. In our current struggles over questions of human sexuality, particularly homosexuality, it is the interpretation of the Scriptures, not their authority, that is at issue. As one who has been ordained four times by the church, once as a Lutheran and three times as an Episcopalian, I have publicly declared each time that I believe the Scriptures of the Old and New Testaments to be the word of God and to contain all things necessary to salvation. I still believe that, and God being my witness, I believe I have been faithful to that declaration. What I do not believe now, and have never believed, is that everything the Bible contains is a matter of salvation. Though some might claim such a belief, I don't think that even the most conservative biblical interpreters believe that everything in the Bible is necessary to salvation.

The rub comes, of course, among good, faithful Episcopalians, all of whom recognize and honor the *authority* of Scripture, but thoughtfully and honestly disagree on the *interpretation* of certain passages. It has helped me to reflect on how my own interpretation of certain passages has changed over the years. One might reasonably ask: How can that be? How can the interpretation of the Scriptures change? I do not argue that the Scriptures change (although biblical scholarship has certainly helped us establish readings of the texts that are closer to the intent of the original biblical writers, and have made it possible to correct some of our misinterpretations of times past due to poor translations). What I do suggest is that *I have changed.* And that is a good thing! And I sincerely believe that such change is a testimony to the power of the risen Christ alive and well in my life and in the life of the church.

Let me offer an example or two. The first Bible verse I ever memorized was John 3:16: "For God so loved the world that he gave his only Son, so that everyone who believes in him may not perish but may have eternal life." I marvel at how my hearing of that passage has changed over the years. From the time I was a young child until partway through my teen years, I heard that passage from the perspective of hellfire and damnation. The words that spoke most clearly were *may not perish.* The text was essentially about fire insurance, about not going to hell, and my Sunday school teachers did everything they could to underscore that interpretation. As an older teenager, more secure in my faith and less marginalized by the church, I began to hear the text differently. I noticed that the words that touched my heart were *God so loved.* They became the foundational text for an ever-deepening sense of the ultimacy of the love of God in all things, at all times. That was a life-changing shift in perspective. Somewhat later, in seminary, I realized once again that my hearing of John 3:16 was shifting. Now the words that caught the attention of my heart were *that he gave.* I began to see in a new way that life in Christ was a precious gift, and perhaps most importantly, a gift of unmerited grace. I began to catch on, in a powerful way, to the heart of the Gospel: All of life and salvation is a gift of God that I cannot earn, but can only enjoy, gracefully and responsively. I've never been the same since. Where am I now? I find myself in yet another place. When I reflect and pray with those familiar words from John's gospel now, what I find most compelling are the words *the world*—all people, all places, all conditions, all—God so loved *all*—everybody. There is no one for whom the Lord has not died.

In one sense that is what we mean when we describe the Bible as the living and dynamic word of God. The text does not change, but how we interact with the text at different times in our lives under the inspiration of the Holy Spirit, how God reveals himself to us differently as we make our way along this journey to Christ, is a powerful testimony to the power of the risen Christ, at work in our hearts and minds and souls. Consider this example from the stories of Jesus.

We all know the story of the prodigal son. It is one of our favorites of Jesus' parables. It is so central to our understanding of God that some biblical theologians have said it is arguably the heart of the good news of Jesus. You remember the story. The younger son goes to his father and begs him for his share of the inheritance. Eventually the father relents, gives the boy his part of the family assets, and the boy sets off to "live it up" away from home. Pretty soon the young man discovers that he has depleted all that his father had given him. He finds himself hungry and homeless, not living even as well as the pigs; which, given the way folks in the Hebrew culture felt about pigs, is not very high on the hog, so to speak. So the younger son, in desperation, comes to his senses and says to himself, "I am going to go to my father and tell him that I have sinned and that I am no longer worthy to be called a son, but maybe he will let me live and eat with the animals." And so he goes to make his confession and beg for his father's mercy. Then comes the best part of the story. As he approaches his father's house, his father sees him coming and runs out to meet him. He embraces his lost son, tells the servants to prepare a feast, sends for the best robe in the house and a new ring for his boy's finger. The father clearly had been waiting and longing for the return of his son. Did you notice that the son never actually got to make the confession that he went home to make? The father was so glad to have his wayward son home that they skipped right past repentance and confession, and immediately got about the business of rejoicing over the one who was gone, but now was home.

Like many, for years I thought this passage was about a wayward son who had squandered his inheritance in loose living, came to his senses, repented, and went home and apologized to his daddy. Now I believe that this is a story about a loving father who let his boy go because his young son needed to grow up. But the father, in his heart, never really let the son go. He stood on the porch day after day, looking down the road with a longing heart and wide-open arms, waiting, longing, hoping that his boy would soon come home. And when he came home, there was no cost, no guilt, no questions asked, but only the welcoming love of a gracious father for his wayward boy. The text hasn't changed, but my understanding, my *interpretation*, of the text has changed enormously. And I am grateful to God for the gift of my conversion, the gift of a changed mind and heart and vision.

It is important to say a little more about the interpretation of Scripture. I think it is fair to suggest that among Christians, there are two extreme positions on biblical interpretation. It is also important to point out that few Christians, if any, live at the extreme ends of the spectrum. (It is clear to me that even some folks who would dogmatically claim to live at one extreme or the other, in fact, do not.) Let's examine both possibilities.

At one end are those who believe that the Bible is the depository of indisputable eternal truths that cannot be questioned or changed. Folks who hold this view often speak in terms of "moral absolutes," which is to say that right is always right, and wrong is always wrong, and there should never be any debate. "Just do what the Bible says," they say, "and don't vary a jot or a tittle from it, and everything will be just fine."

At the other end are those who believe that the Bible is not a book of moral absolutes; it is not a rule book whose primary purpose is to delineate do's and don'ts, rights and wrongs. This side would say that the main purpose of the Bible is to make it clear just how much God loves us, the lengths to which God is willing to go to love us, and that God's love is available to us just as we are. This side concedes that there are lots of "laws" in the Bible, but that such laws are there to demonstrate how impossible it is for sinful human beings ever to get it right, and thereby salvation has to come as a gift of God by the power of the cross and resurrection of Jesus.

Obviously there is truth to both sides, at both extremes, but I don't believe that the people of God have had much success at living for long at either one of those polar positions. As always, I believe that the truth we are meant to grasp is somewhere in the middle; that the truth we seek comes from holding the extremes in tension and living in that tension—not trying, as so many do, to make the tension go away. Here's how I would describe it.

The Scriptures of the Old and New Testament are first and foremost the narrative of how God has dealt with his people through thousands of years, in a variety of cultures, and in response to an array of often difficult conditions. At the heart of the story is God's challenge to the people to accept and live according to a clear sense of moral responsibility—*the law*. But this same story repeatedly demonstrates God's love and forgiveness when the people, individually or corporately, fail to live up to the expectations that God has set forth—*the gospel.* I believe, for example, that the Bible sets forth standards of life and behavior, but I do not believe that the book is fundamentally a "rule book." It is, instead, the story of God and God's people. Its primary character is not "I," and the story line is not principally about how "I" should behave. The primary character is God, and the story line is primarily about how God has acted, how God has responded, how God has been made incarnate in Jesus Christ, and how a risen and living Lord continues today to lead us into all truth by the power of the Holy Spirit (John 14:25–26).

Now let's ask a few questions about "eternal truths." If the Scriptures proclaim something that was clearly true for the biblical writers, must it always and forever be true? Specifically, must it be true for us? (Here it might be good to take a few minutes away from this text and, to gain a sense of perspective, read again the opening verses of Ecclesiastes, chapter 3.)

Back in the first chapter of Genesis, in the story about God's creation of the world, we are told in verse 28: "Be fruitful and multiply, and fill the earth and subdue it." That verse clearly has meant a great deal to the community of faith at certain times and places. The nomadic people of the Hebrews, for example, were settling down to a different kind of lifestyle in Canaan. They had enemies on all sides. They consequently needed people: more men to be soldiers and more women to have babies, who would grow up and be soldiers or grow up and mother that many more. But what about now? Do we continue to take seriously God's charge that we be fruitful and multiply in an age that is marked by severe overpopulation and a serious worldwide shortage of safe drinking water, and in which thousands of children die *every day* of starvation? I don't think so. I do believe that there is serious *theological truth* in the early chapters of Genesis, which continues to teach and inspire us, but reason will not allow me to embrace Genesis 1:28 as God's command to us in our time and under present global conditions.

And let's remind ourselves of a couple of New Testament examples. In 1 Corinthians, chapter 11, when Saint Paul is instructing the church on the proper way to live together, he says that women should cover their heads in church. He never actually tells us why this should be the case. Was it a practical matter, like a sunbonnet, or simply a reflection of middle eastern culture, like the *hijab* worn by women in many Islamic countries today? It may be as simple as distinguishing "Christian" women from their pagan counterparts. For many years, of course (as many of us still recall), women always wore hats to church, ostensibly in obedience to this injunction of Saint Paul's. But times have changed, haven't they? Today it is a rare woman in any of our parishes who covers her head in church, and most of us don't give it a second thought. If you want to be literal about it, bareheaded women in church are violating biblical teaching.

In not a dissimilar fashion, a few chapters later, in 1 Corinthians, chapter 14, Saint Paul says that women should be silent in church. That prohibition almost surely reflects the fact that the culture of Paul's time was heavily patriarchal. Women were the property of their fathers and then of their husbands. They possessed no rights of their own, and therefore had no voice worthy of being heard. For centuries the church colluded with that position. Women were denied any public voice in the church. Only men could be priests, and only laymen, never laywomen, were admitted to the councils of the church. It has not been that many years since our own Episcopal Church admitted women to serve as deputies at the General Convention, and changed the canons so that women could serve as members of parish vestries. And, of course, it is only since 1976 that women have been eligible to serve in this church as deacons, priests, and bishops. All this is in direct opposition to the directives of Saint Paul. I, for one, am glad we see things a little differently than he did. I can't imagine where we would be without the gracious and powerful presence of women in the total life of the church. May their tribe increase.

I do not give those examples to trivialize the important questions before us, but to remind us that to some degree the human writers of the sacred texts were discerning God's will through the lenses of their own time and place, their own culture and circumstances. That does not mean, in my mind, that such passages are to be taken lightly or ignored. Often profound theological truth is found "beneath the surface" of the literal reading, and that truth is more important to us than the surface truth in developing our understanding of God and God's desire for us. I also raise these points because I believe we would all concede that there are passages in Scripture that we overlook and no longer take seriously.

The hard part comes in distinguishing what to take seriously and what not to. Again, let's look at some examples.

In the Old Testament book of Leviticus, the ancient community is trying to work out the practical implications of the Ten Commandments—to apply the fundamental truths of the Ten Commandments to the details of daily living, the ten "big ones" into over six hundred "little ones." Much of this we recognize and still honor without hesitation. For example, in Leviticus 19:11 we read, "You shall not steal; you shall not deal falsely; and you shall not lie to one another." That's a clear summary of two of the commandments. Who is prepared to disagree with either one? I'm not. A little later, however, in verse 19, things get a bit more complicated: "You shall not let your animals breed with a different kind; you shall not sow your field with two kinds of seed; nor shall you put on a garment made of two different materials." Well, there go the mules! (Mules are a crossbreed of donkeys and horses.) And so much for all those farms in Peach County, Georgia, where peaches and pecans grow side by side. And there go all my wool-blend suits right out the window. Obviously, we take some verses quite differently than we take others.

The questions around divorce and adultery are interesting ones. The law of God as interpreted by the Old Testament writers makes provision for divorce (Deuteronomy, chapter 24), but it seems to apply only to a man who finds something objectionable about his wife. This bias toward the male is completely understandable in a culture in which women were the property of men, and thereby could be discarded at will. Jesus, by contrast, has strong words about divorce, and clearly does not give the wiggle room that one finds in the Old Testament (Mark 10:1–12). Unlike the Old Testament, Jesus does seem to concede that a woman may give her husband a writ of divorce, so by Jesus' time it appears that the application of the law was more balanced than in earlier times. A broader interpretation of those passages suggests to me that Jesus was raising the standard of women (acknowledging their right to give their husbands a writ of divorce), and his strong teaching against divorce was directed at the men of his day who were far too quick to dispense with their wives on a whim. In other words, Jesus was raising the ante on the mutuality of the covenant of marriage, and telling the men that it was not acceptable to treat their wives as disposable property.

I have always found it interesting that most Christians prefer the Old Testament view of divorce over the view set forth by Jesus, which is much stricter and more forbidding. But in either case, one who is divorced and marries another is without question an adulterer, a sin that is punishable by death (Deuteronomy, chapter 22). Perhaps it is because approximately half of the marriages in the general population end in divorce (and the statistics for churchgoers fall in the same range) that we find it easier to set aside the prohibitions against divorce and ignore the fact that adultery, by biblical standards, demands capital punishment.

The most severe reading of the prohibitive texts in the Bible on same-sex behavior takes the same position on that behavior as it does on adultery—it is an abomination, and it is punishable by death. Isn't it interesting that one abomination (adultery) no longer phases most people, but the other abomination (same-sex behavior) is still a severe taboo? The church's response to divorce and adultery is clear. We believe it is the breaking of a sacred covenant; it is sin, plain and simple. But taking our cue from Jesus, we also believe that all are sinners and in need of redemption and healing. So we counsel with pastoral care and therapy those of our brothers and sisters whose marriages are coming apart. We insist on the proper care and nurture of any children born to the union. We do not allow our people to remarry until such time that the church is convinced that amendment of life, increased maturity, and confession and absolution have made visible a more faithful life. I believe that our church continues to take marriage with utter seriousness. Our clergy spend many hours in pastoral care of divorcing or divorced persons. We name the reality of their lives as sinful, but we forgive them in the name of Jesus, love them back into spiritual health, and welcome them into the full life of the church, including the ordained ministry.

The interpretation of Holy Scripture is a difficult task. If the foregoing pages prove nothing else, they indicate a variety of ways to interpret the most important texts of our life together as Christian people. Perhaps Saint Paul can help us one last time before we turn directly to the biblical texts on same-sex behavior. I don't think anyone believes that Saint Paul was a libertarian who advocated an "anything goes" philosophy (as long as it doesn't hurt someone else). He was, in fact, one who "leaned to the right," and his advice and counsel generally called for restraint, if not prohibition. Yet this same Paul, whose theology became the centerpiece of the Protestant Reformation in the sixteenth century, was crystal clear in his teaching about justification. A person is justified before God, Paul wrote, *not* by works of the law (that is, not by how successful one is in following the law) *but only by faith in Jesus Christ* (Romans 3:20,28; Galatians 2:16). The righteousness we all desire is of Christ, a gift of God, and does not come by way of the law (Romans 4:13, Galatians 3:18). Because of the sacrificial death and glorious resurrection of Jesus Christ, we are no longer under law, but we are now under grace (Romans 6:14). The law has given way to Christ (Romans 10:4). Under Christ the law can no longer give life (Galatians 3:21).

According to the teachings of Saint Paul, the law is superceded and summarized by the commandment to love one's neighbor as oneself (Galatians 5:14). In Romans, Paul provides a summary of his thinking that is almost identical to the teachings of Jesus in Matthew 22:39–40 and John 13:34. Paul writes:

> *Owe no one anything, except to love one another; for the one who loves another has fulfilled the law. The commandments, "You shall not commit adultery; You shall not murder; You shall not steal; You shall not covet"; and any other commandment, are summed up in this word, "Love your neighbor as yourself." Love does no wrong to a neighbor; therefore, love is the fulfilling of the law. (13:8–10)*

It goes without saying that what we mean by the word *love* is sometimes nothing more than a mushy sentiment. Jesus and Paul had more than that in mind. I believe that Jesus and Paul were arguing in favor of appropriate standards of Christian behavior. I believe that their point is that love is a "higher standard," a more difficult, more demanding way. To retreat to the law, on this side of the resurrection of Jesus, is to take the easy way out. The saving work of God in Christ has dethroned the law. Love, made incarnate in Jesus, has been put in its place. The law still has its usefulness—it is God's own gift to us—but the ultimate law for the Christian is the law of love. Jesus, remember, was short-tempered with the good and faithful Pharisees who were more interested in the meticulous keeping of certain laws to the point that they were blind to what was important, the "weightier" matters" of justice, mercy, and faith (Matthew 23:23–24).

The Bible and Same-Sex Behavior

Only a handful of Bible passages, mostly single verses, are generally recognized to be related to the subject of same-sex behavior. Given the fact that same-sex behavior was well known in the ancient world, it is more than a little puzzling that the Bible doesn't talk more about it, and more clearly about it, especially if its position on the matter is to be construed as negative in all circumstances. In discussions of this difficult subject through the years, I find it amazing how Christians resort all too often to tossing Bible verses as if they were hand grenades, attempting to hurt one another with the word of God. I would prefer that we break open the texts in their fullness and listen to one another about how the Spirit may be speaking to us through the word. What follows is my imperfect attempt to break open and listen to the sacred texts.

Sodom and Gibeah

Two stories in the Old Testament are generally understood to be relevant to the matter before us: Genesis 19:1–14 (the destruction of Sodom) and Judges 19:1–30 (the concubine at Gibeah). Most biblical scholars believe that these two stories are essentially the same, having emerged from common sources within the ancient tradition. They appear in the biblical text as two versions of the same story. The details have changed over time, as always happens in stories that circulate for a long time in oral tradition. The stories have, as it were, been locally adapted. Here we will look at each one separately.

Genesis 19:1–14

This passage is part of a larger narrative that includes a number of stories of Abraham and his nephew, Lot. *Before* we get to chapter 19, God had decided already to destroy Sodom (Genesis 18:16–21). Part of the story is the bargaining that goes on between God and Abraham about whether there are enough faithful left in Sodom to spare the city (Genesis 18:22–32). (It is interesting to note that God here seems to be listening to Abraham's thoughts on the matter. This classical biblical passage seems to suggest that sinful human beings might, in fact, have some influence on God!) So God sends two messengers to see if things are really as bad in Sodom as has been reported. When the messengers arrive, they meet Lot, and what is not immediately apparent is that he, like them, is a visitor to the city. The messengers intended simply to spend the night sleeping in the town square, but Lot persuades them to be his guests. The invitation will later turn out to be a problem, because Lot himself is an "alien," and according to the customs of the time, a guest cannot provide hospitality to other guests because that deprives citizens of the opportunity to provide hospitality themselves.

In time the citizens of Sodom discover that the messengers—the guests—are not staying among their own, but with Lot—another guest. They immediately wonder what's up, and seek out the guests at Lot's quarters. Given the fact that the city is about to be under siege, it is not hard to imagine that the people of Sodom were more than a little anxious about any aliens in their territory who chose to stay, not among the citizenry, but with other visitors. Were they spies? Were they plotting? Who were these messengers? So the men of Sodom track them down and demand "to know" them.

In Hebrew the verb *to know* is a tricky one. Every priest on the first day of seminary learns that "to know" refers to knowing another in the most intimate way possible: to have sexual intercourse. While this *can* be true, it is at least as likely that it is a distortion of the meaning of the text. By my count there are 943 uses of the Hebrew "to know," and 933—all but ten uses—mean exactly what we would mean when we used the verb "to know": personal knowledge that bears with it no intent or assumption of sexual intimacy. So, while "to know" *could* refer to sexual intimacy, it is at least as likely that it means that the local folks of Sodom wanted to know who those guys were, what their business in town was, where they were from, when they were leaving, and why they were shunning the local population and its hospitality by hiding out with another alien.

Whatever it was that the locals wanted to know, it is clear that they were offended. Why? We don't know for sure, but it is entirely plausible that the anger and offense of the men of Sodom was that their cultural conventions had been violated by Lot—a visitor usurping the privilege of hospitality that rightly belonged only to the local folks. When the angry mob becomes confrontational, Lot finds himself in a difficult spot. He has extended hospitality to the strangers—something that was not his to give—and therefore he has an obligation to protect those who have come under his roof. When the men of Sodom demand to see the strangers, Lot tries to bargain with the only chips he has available, his virgin daughters. That's a hard pill for many of us in this culture to swallow. I can't imagine taking in some strangers, having the police knock on the door and ask for them, and telling the police that I had an obligation to protect those strangers, but if they wanted, they could have my children. Yet if one studies the culture of biblical times, one comes to realize that "hospitality to the stranger" was not simply a matter of gracious helpfulness. It was a matter of life and death. You were obligated above all to care for your guests because of the likelihood that, on another day, you will be the guest and will require water, food, shelter, and protection. As horrifying as it may seem to us, the people of ancient times were willing to put themselves and their children in harm's way if it meant keeping the honor of their guests.

An interesting story that sheds light on this is found in Joshua, chapter 6, the story of Rahab at the conquest of Jericho. In preparation for the great battle, Joshua sends spies into the city to gather intelligence. The spies find refuge in the home of Rahab, the town prostitute. Before the final siege of the city, Joshua sends two of his men to retrieve Rahab and her family so they will be spared when the town is destroyed. Why? Why spare the town harlot? *Because she offered hospitality to the strangers, and was thereby deemed worthy of being spared when the rest of Jericho was destroyed.*

Many scholars who have studied Genesis, chapter 19 believe that what caused the ruckus in Sodom was the violation of the mandatory social conventions of hospitality. Without diminishing the importance of that interpretation, some continue to insist that there is more sexual content here than the interpretation allows, noting specifically Lot's response to give his virgin daughters for the men of Sodom "to do to them as [they] please." In other words, why would Lot offer his daughters for sex if that's not what the men of Sodom were looking for? And why did they insist on getting to the men behind Lot's door if they were not interested in sex with them? Those questions are fair enough, and I can certainly understand why one might want to read it that way. But it is also clear from the text that if the men of Sodom wanted same-sex relations, they wanted them *by force,* not by mutual consent. Their reaction is obviously one of anger and rage with violent intent. Therefore it would seem that the intent was not consensual same-sex relations, but gang rape. Most of us would agree, I believe, that rape is not a matter of sex; it is a matter of violence. Rape was wrong in Sodom. Rape is wrong now. Rape will always be wrong. It is therefore quite possible to read this passage as a condemnation of violence (even with its sexual connotations), and not as a condemnation of sexuality, faithfully and lovingly expressed.

It is also important to read Genesis, chapter 19, against the backdrop of Genesis 18:16–32. The side-by-side narratives demonstrate the tension in which the people of God always find themselves living: the tension between *faith* and *sin.* That tension is made palpable in the proximity of the story of the faith of Abraham (Genesis, chapter 18), and the story of the sins of Sodom (Genesis, chapter 19). The tension between faith and sin is ever present in the whole of the biblical story, but the tension always finds its release in faith, the taproot of God's justice, mercy, and love.

The context of the story, the use of the Hebrew verb *to know,* the severe restrictions and conventions governing hospitality in the ancient world, the fact that Lot's daughters were the only bargaining chips he had, and that he was morally obligated *to do anything* to protect his guests, are, on balance, at least as plausible an interpretation of the text as seeing it as an episode of perverse sexual behavior among men. If it *was* that, I believe we must all agree that it was an attempted homosexual rape—something of which I trust that none of us approve—and not loving, consensual sexual relations between persons of the same sex. That's a big difference.

So what was the sin of Sodom? The Bible does not spell it out in Genesis, chapter 19. The fact that many see it as same-sex behavior ultimately is not helpful to us. At most one might be able to argue that some sort of same-sex violence was among the sins of Sodom that were displeasing to God. There are too many references to Sodom in the Old and New Testaments to review every one of them here, so a few examples will have to suffice.

In the passage itself, verse 13 is interesting: "For we are about to destroy this place, because the outcry against its people has become great before the LORD, and the LORD has sent us to destroy it." The key word here is *outcry*, which is generally an interpretive tip-off that the root of the problem has something to do with a violation of justice, particularly God's justice. Assuming that this is the situation in Sodom, the text then has no need to single out sexual sin from among other possibilities to make the point. Other passages that note the sins of Sodom refer to a veritable laundry list of things that God finds displeasing: spiritual apathy and casualness (Isaiah 1:9–10); adultery and lying (Jeremiah, chapter 14); those who feast when children are hungry (Lamentations 4:5–6); haughtiness, pride, excess food, prosperous ease, failure to support the poor and needy (Ezekiel 16:48–55).

In the New Testament, Jesus says that a town that fails to welcome the stranger—those who are sent to us in the name of Jesus—will suffer the same fate as Sodom (Matthew 10:14–15, 11:23–24; Luke 10:12, 17:29). This is a teaching that ought to be of great concern to us in the present moment. Another New Testament reference to Sodom, 2 Peter 2:8, gives no indication of the sin of Sodom. Only Jude, verse 7, of all the texts I can find, seems to suggest that same-sex behavior was the principal infraction of God's will in Sodom. Overall, however, it seems that the sins of Sodom were many in number and not limited to sins of the flesh, heterosexual or homosexual, and that some sort of violent same-sex behavior is clearly only one among the sins in which God takes displeasure.

JUDGES 19:1–30

As noted previously, this story is largely parallel to the story of Sodom. It is quite likely that it has a common source in the oral tradition and that its details have been adapted to its audience over a period of time. As the story goes, a Levite (of the priestly order) is on his way home to Bethlehem with his concubine and a servant. They stop and spend the night in the town of Gibeah. They are offered the customary hospitality of the time, taken in, and given the necessary provisions, shelter, and protection.

In the course of the night, "a perverse lot" of men of the city come and demand to see the guest, ostensibly to have forced sexual relations with him. The master of the house refuses to put his guest in harm's way and offers both his own virgin daughter and his guest's concubine: "Ravish them and do whatever you want to them" (verse 24). The wicked men of Gibeah "wantonly raped" the concubine "and abused her all through the night until the morning" (verse 25).

It is clear that the wicked men of Gibeah wanted violent same-sex relations with a visitor to their city, a passerby who was rightfully protected from such abuse by his host. The host fulfilled his social and cultural obligations by providing both his daughter and his friend's concubine, the latter of whom was raped repeatedly through the course of the night. It is difficult to read the host's protection of his guest from gang rape by a group of wicked men as an indictment of consensual, loving relationships between persons of the same sex. The host had a social and cultural obligation to protect his guest, even if it meant that the concubine had to face the humiliation of being raped again and again by a gang of wicked men. In the next chapter (20:6), the people of Israel rise up and make war against the citizens of Gibeah. Why? Not because of some same-sex incident that never actually took place, but because of the violent rape of an innocent woman by angry, wicked, out-of-control men. To conclude that anything from this passage is relevant to our present conversations in the church concerning homosexuality seems to me a significant stretch.

LEVITICUS 18:22, 20:13

In chapters 17 through 26 of the book of Leviticus, we find a lengthy catalogue of the rules and regulations intended *for the people of Israel* (see the note at the beginning of almost every chapter of Leviticus—17:2, 18:2, 19:2, and so on), and for their priests (22:2, 23:2). This catalogue is generally referred to in biblical studies as the "holiness code," and is thought of as the practical application of God's law agreed on by the people of that time and place. In some ways the holiness code is Israel's working out of the details of common life, similar to the way in which the constitution of a nation or the canons of a church work out how people of their own time and place intend to live together. Some verses of the holiness code reflect the people's allegiance to the primacy of the Ten Commandments. Other verses clearly reflect the social customs, ritual practices, and cultural biases of the time.

It has been customary among Christians to study the holiness code in Leviticus, and to discover how God's people of another time and place tried to work out the details of living together as people of faith. In that sense the texts continue to instruct us. However, even among the most conservative interpreters of the Bible, most will say that the holiness code no longer applies to us in the same way that it did to the people of ancient times. The Ten Commandments, on which it is based, certainly apply, but the practical details are those of another time and place, for those who were working out their common life under the Old Covenant, and such details are not directly relevant to those of us who live by the power of the resurrection of Jesus under the New Covenant of love and reconciliation. It is interesting that we are nearly unanimous in the dismissal of the holiness code as it applies to those of us who live on this side of the resurrection, except for two verses that appear to address the question of same-sex behavior, Leviticus 18:22 and 20:13. Those texts are nearly identical, so we will examine them together.

Both of those texts make the same essential point: that a man shall not lie with another man as with a woman. Setting aside the fact that it is impossible to start with, the text must have a deeper meaning that is not immediately apparent.

We are also told that such behavior is an abomination. Perhaps that is the place to begin our investigation. The Hebrew word that is translated as "abomination" is most often understood to be cultic in its field of meaning, and is not used to connote moral content. In other words, the abomination is precisely that, not because it is inherently immoral but because it is offensive with respect to the cultic requirements of Israel's faith. Israel was but one of many faiths of the Middle East, and some other faiths featured sexual activities as typical facets of their cultic life. I think we can all agree that many sexual practices are acceptable and moral, but that the doing of them in the midst of our own cultic life would be offensive, inappropriate in the extreme, and therefore an abomination. We don't have sex of any kind *in church!* I think we can all agree with the writer of Leviticus that men having sex with men as with a woman (or any other combination of sexual partners) is unacceptable— an abomination—as part of our religious rituals. (Remember, the entirety of the book of Leviticus is about the regulation of worship in Israel.)

Today's questions are quite different. Same-sex behavior, or any-sex behavior, within the Christian tradition is not a part of the liturgy. If the Leviticus texts carry with them no *moral* objection, but only *cultic* ones, then this passage is not, in the end, very helpful to us. That is even more the case if we remember the ease with which even the most conservative interpreters of the Bible would de-emphasize the largest part of the holiness code, *except* for those two verses.

If, however, one finds the distinction between the moral and the cultic unhelpful, then perhaps those two verses can be heard alongside the other verses in the holiness code that are concerned with other sexual behaviors—Leviticus 18:19, 18:20, 20:10, 20:11, 20:12, 20:14. Most of those statements refer to one or another liaison that would come under the general heading of adultery, the preeminent heterosexual abomination that is punishable by death.

The fact that the Levitical indictment renders guilty somewhat more than half of the population, and sentences them to death, seems of little consequence to most of us today. I do not believe that it is because we fail to take marriage and its covenants with utter seriousness, in the church at least. I believe that the teachings of Jesus and the power of the resurrection allow us to see things differently. The power of love transcends the sin of adultery. What we desire for such sinners is not death but forgiveness, a new beginning, and the chance to have a whole, life-giving, sacramental relationship in which God is vitally present. That is precisely the sort of relationship that is also the desire and longing of our gay and lesbian brothers and sisters.

Another aspect of those verses needs to be noted. It is, I confess, the most compelling argument for me personally. If we yield the fact that same-sex relations between men were despised by those of ancient times, we might ask if there is another reason they felt strongly about it. I think there is.

In the ancient, prescientific world, people believed that male sperm was the source of life. They did not know of the female ovum. They thought of women simply as passive incubators of the life that had been deposited within them. The reproductive mystery of sperm and egg was outside of the framework of their understanding. It is rather easy, therefore, to imagine how protective they would be of male sperm. In like manner, it is not unreasonable to suggest that the anxiety in the ancient world about same-sex relations between men emerges from the same concerns. Because one's male sexual partner cannot incubate the sperm and produce a life, the sperm is wasted. Such a waste of life is to be despised. In a society under threat, in which continued growth of the population is vital to the survival of the nation, it is easy to see how a concern for protecting the gift of life would be paramount in all circumstances. Interestingly, there appear to be no prohibitions of female same-sex relationships. Why? Was it because women in the ancient world were not attracted to each other and because same-sex behavior was only a male phenomenon? I don't think so. I am inclined to believe that such prohibitions do not exist because women were not understood to have an active role in reproduction. They did not bear in their bodies the gift of life; they only incubated the life that the dominant male placed within them. Female same-sex relationships therefore were not a threat to the stability and continuity of the community.

JESUS

I have often wondered why Jesus had nothing to say about same-sex behavior. He had lots of things to say about self-righteousness. He never missed a chance to point out to those who were hell-bent on keeping the details of the Levitical laws that they better get the log out of their own eye before they tried to remove the speck from their neighbor's. He chided the Pharisees about getting so engrossed in trapping others in the legalities of life that they were blinded to the "weightier" matters of God's mercy, justice, and love. It's not that Jesus did not have high standards of behavior for those whom he called to follow him. It's certainly not that Jesus did not have a moral vision for living faithfully as servants of God. Yet he neither says nor even implies a single syllable about same-sex behavior. That makes me curious.

How can that be? Some might suggest that Jesus did not say anything about same-sex behavior because everything that needed to be said had already been said. That's not a very satisfying answer when you think about the fact that Jesus doesn't hold back anywhere else. Why would he hold back on this topic? Perhaps Jesus found the subject distasteful and not proper for polite conversation. But that never stopped him before!

The fact is that it is impossible to know why Jesus never spoke to the issue. But maybe we can find a clue.

We have long known that same-sex behavior was well known (and not a secret) in the Greek and Roman world at the time of Jesus. The Roman emperors had same-sex lovers in addition to their wives and concubines. The poets of the era, both Roman and Greek, exalt the joys of same-sex love. The historical record suggests that same-sex behavior was an accepted part of the prevailing culture. That fact alone, of course, does not make it right in the eyes of God or the faith community, but its wide acceptance does provide Jesus every possible opportunity and reason to condemn it if that's what he wants to do. He could not have had a clearer target. Yet, so far as we know, he never rose to the occasion.

Do we know why? No. But here is a clue. We have noted that adultery gets far more attention in the Bible than does same-sex behavior. We know, however, that Jesus reached out and accepted an adulterous woman, and charged her accusers with the words, "Let anyone among you who is without sin be the first to throw a stone at her" (John 8:7). If adultery is seen as at least as severe as same-sex behavior, if not more so, and if Jesus accepts the woman who is caught in adultery and dismisses her accusers, then is it possible that Jesus accepts people who engage in same-sex behavior as well? We cannot know for sure, but the possibility is worth considering. Given the larger context of the ministry of Jesus—his clear love for prostitutes, outcasts, and sinners of all sorts—perhaps it is not all that surprising that Jesus did not single out those who engaged in same-sex behavior as being in any way different from the pack of all sinners who were in need of redeeming grace and loving acceptance. In fact, it is not unreasonable to suggest that Jesus focuses on adultery because it results in greater damage to the societal family fabric than would consensual same-sex behavior.

Paul

Three passages from Saint Paul (or his "school of thought") require our attention. Each of these texts has its own purpose and its own context in the story of the New Testament, and each is directed to a particular community of faith that is in fellowship with their apostle, Paul. It is important to emphasize that in all the letters of Saint Paul, we often are witnesses to an ongoing conversation between the apostle and his community, and if you jump into the text without understanding where you are in the unfolding conversation, you can understand Paul to be saying something quite different from what he is actually saying. These three examples demonstrate well the problem and challenge faced by any who are interpreting Scripture today.

Romans 1:26–27. The larger argument of Paul to the church at Rome is about the grace of God, which comes by faith in Jesus Christ. Grace is not earned by keeping the works of the law, because in the resurrection of Christ, a new day, a new covenant, and a new way of being have come to pass. There are those in the first-century Roman church who are clearly stuck on good works and the keeping of the law of the Old Covenant, and Paul is working hard to convince them that, although keeping some aspects of the law may well continue to be good for them, salvation—being in right relationship with God—is not a matter of keeping the law but a matter of faith in Jesus Christ, itself a gift of God's merciful grace by the power of the Holy Spirit. To understand the first stage of Paul's argument, it is essential not to dwell on two verses— 1:26–27—but to read carefully the entirety of the first three chapters of Romans, and to allow 1:26–27 to be seen in the larger context of Paul's complete argument.

For the sake of clarity, here's a stab at how that argument unfolds. Paul begins by observing that if people are alienated from God, the reason is that God "gave them up." Why did God do this? God gave them up *because they exercised their own will and turned away from the Creator,* exchanging the truth of God for the worship of idols. In other words, God gave them up not because God was not faithful, not because God desired to turn away, *but because the people chose to turn away.*

Then Paul's argument takes an important turn. The fact that people are separated from God is, in Paul's mind, proven by the fact that they engage in improper conduct. God has not given people up because the people have engaged in improper conduct; rather, their improper conduct proves that they have turned away from God.

Let's put that a slightly different way. The people are separated from God *not* because of their improper conduct but because *they have chosen* to separate themselves from God. The proof of that separation is to be found in their improper conduct. That may seem like a distinction without a difference—splitting hairs—but it is precisely the distinction that Paul is making, and it is critical to understanding where Paul's argument is going. Without such a distinction, it will be impossible for Paul to get to where he wants to go in his argument in later chapters.

The proof of separation from God is not limited to 1:26–27. Paul develops a long, but surely incomplete, list of vices—"every kind of wickedness"—evil, covetousness, malice, envy, murder, strife, deceit, gossip, slander, haughtiness, disobedience to parents, foolishness, faithlessness, heartlessness, and ruthlessness (1:28–31). And, Paul declares, all such vices deserve capital punishment (1:32).

So what is Paul's point? Paul sees clearly that if we depend on keeping the law, we are all doomed. As he will point out at the summit of his argument, "all have sinned and fall short of the glory of God" (Romans 3:23). In the first two chapters, Paul is wearing down the church at Rome, with despair over their inability as human beings to keep the law (and thereby escape capital punishment), so that he can proclaim to them all the more boldly that *all people* are justified before God, *not* by works of the law, but by *saving grace* appropriated by faith in Jesus Christ (3:24–25). This is the teaching that Paul is trying to drive home to the church at Rome. The core of Paul's teaching is that we are saved by God's free gift, unmerited and unearned, and accessed through faith in Jesus Christ, itself a gift of the Holy Spirit. The gift of God's mercy and grace is for all—*everybody*—not of our own deserving, but precisely because we don't deserve it. Otherwise it wouldn't be grace at all.

But for the record, let's isolate 1:26–27 for closer examination. These are hard texts, and, as usual, there is probably a great deal more going on here than meets the eye in a surface reading of the English text. In 1:26 Paul says, "Their women exchanged natural intercourse for unnatural." Is that a reference to women having same-sex relations? It could be understood that way on the basis of the English text alone, but I believe it probably has to do with the customs of the times and the people's understanding of human reproduction, not dissimilar to our earlier discussion of Leviticus. It seems entirely plausible to understand "unnatural intercourse" as a reference to those sexual practices that the Jewish tradition at the time of Paul (remember, Paul was a Jew) believed to be "unnatural" precisely because they did not end up in the conception and nurture of new life. The importance of this for the maintenance of their society has been noted previously. We know, for example, that the Jews of Paul's day rejected heterosexual practices such as coitus interruptus, anal intercourse, and a female taking the superior position; those practices were considered "unnatural" for the simple reason that they did not lead to babies. There is no need therefore to interpret this verse as referring to same-sex behavior between women.

Verse 27 is a little more complicated. It is quite clear that Paul is talking here about same-sex behavior between men. I don't think there is any way around that. But we do ourselves a disservice if we fail to dig a little deeper into what is lurking beneath the text. The primary question for me is this: Does Paul summarily condemn *all* same-sex behavior, or is this a reference to particular behaviors that are not evident in the text?

A momentary divergence, please. One of the first lessons I learned about the interpretation of the letters of Paul is that we always have to keep in mind that they are just that, letters. We all know that letters exchanged between two people who are familiar to each other often use shorthand references, and sometimes no direct references at all, because the writers are involved in an ongoing conversation and do not need to spell out all the details. In studying Paul's letters, biblical scholars spend a great deal of time trying to understand what Paul *does not say* (what he assumes his readers already know), so that we can more clearly understand what he means by what he *does say*. Romans is a letter of Paul's to the church at Rome about specific concerns in their common life. Paul is speaking to concrete situations there. We assume that those who received the letter knew immediately what Paul was talking about; the context of the conversation already had been established. In a real sense, the letter picks up a conversation that already is in progress, as part of the ongoing relationship between the faith community in Rome and their beloved apostle.

What, then, are some of the things that Paul is assuming his community already knows? That's a tough one, and I suspect that we never will know for sure. One explanation is that Paul is referring, in verse 27, not to same-sex behavior in general, but to a specific form of it, well known among the Romans, that Paul found detestable. It was common in those days, and generally accepted, for men (who understood themselves to be heterosexuals) to have a boy for their sexual pleasure. Such relationships were not understood to take the place of women as the principal source of sexual pleasure, but rather to be an additional item on the sexual menu. So common was this practice that evidence suggests that young boys who were not chosen as the companion of an older man were thought to be "unformed," and would therefore not grow up to be a "normal" man. I suspect that you, like me, find this disgusting, and for that reason, I can imagine that Paul found it pretty disgusting, too. Is that what Paul is referring to in 1:27? We can't say for sure, but plenty of biblical scholars have looked at the evidence, both inside the text and in the context to which the text was addressed, and are willing to see that interpretation as a real possibility. If that interpretation is within the realm of plausibility, then I agree wholeheartedly with Paul. It is not appropriate for older men to have young boys as sexual playthings. It wasn't right in Paul's day. It is not right now. It never will be. Case closed.

Is there another interpretation of this text that might help us? Perhaps. I have struggled many years with another interpretation, and only recently have I begun to accept its basic premise. Paul's basic notion is that it is not good for people to give up the natural for the unnatural. Specifically, in verse 27, men are not to give up what is natural (sex with women) for what is unnatural (sex with men). That seems clear enough. But this reading makes a number of assumptions.

I think nearly everyone would agree that, in Paul's day, there was no concept of homosexuality as a "state of life," or as we say today, "sexual orientation." Clearly a great deal of same-sex behavior was going on, and such behavior was regularly thought of as unnatural because the only concept they knew was what we now call heterosexuality. (It is important to remember that the terms *heterosexuality* and *homosexuality* were coined in the psychiatric and medical communities in the late nineteenth century. No such concepts existed in Paul's day.) So, if there is no such thing as homosexuality, only well-known and generally accepted same-sex behavior, then Paul could not be talking here about the same thing that we understand to be homosexuality. Paul, in fact, is quite right to suggest that a heterosexual man having sex with another heterosexual man is without question unnatural. It is, without doubt, a perversion.

Today, however, most of us believe that there is such a thing as homosexuality. Most of us believe that homosexuality is a sexual orientation that a small percentage of the population, male and female, is born to. Most of us no longer believe that homosexuality is a *moral choice*, but is simply the way that God has made some of us, and, further, that God desires fellowship with all of us, homosexual as well as heterosexual.

Earlier in my ordained ministry, I was among those who believed that a person could be healed from homosexuality and restored to the heterosexual lifestyle that was intended for them. I no longer, in good conscience, can believe that. I have known too many homosexual persons for whom sexual orientation clearly was *not* a choice. In some cases they went through years of denial and shame about how God made them. They tried therapy, healing ministry, and a host of reparative strategies, but in the end they have yielded their lives to two facts: God made them homosexual. God loves them just as they are.

So back to Paul. I think the apostle is quite right to suggest that a person should not have sex in an unnatural way, which means that heterosexual persons should not have homosexual sex. Right on, Paul! In the same way, homosexual persons should not have unnatural sex either. They should not act sexually as though they are heterosexuals. The perversion that Paul rightly finds disgusting is simply doing that which is unnatural. I agree.

As a brief aside, I think this gives us some insight into the profoundly emotional, often visceral reaction that many people have to same-sex behavior. We react as we do precisely because it is unnatural to us—we find the thought of it disgusting—and that's as it should be, precisely because we are wonderfully and *differently* made. As a heterosexual male, I react to what is for me the unnaturalness of same-sex behavior. That's the way I am wired. But I have come to appreciate that my homosexual brothers and sisters feel precisely the same way I do on this point: they find their relationships as natural as can be, and can't quite understand my sexual attraction to persons of the opposite sex.

1 Corinthians 6:9–20. Here Saint Paul is writing to the church in Corinth, a community well known in his day as a hot bed of immorality.

The church there was surrounded by moral laxity, and we can infer from Paul's letter that he has evidence that members of the Corinthian church are participating, at some level, in the depravity of the larger culture. Paul's intention in this letter is to remind them of their higher calling as servants of Jesus Christ. He frames the whole letter between the cross (chapter 1) and the resurrection (chapter 15), and the climax of the letter comes into focus in chapter 13, Paul's doxological heartsong on Christian love. Paul knows, however, that the Corinthian Christians are not going to be able to avoid daily contact with nonbelieving neighbors whose lives are characterized by greed, idolatry, drunkenness, and robbery, to mention just a few of their many vices. Furthermore, Paul does not consider it his responsibility to stand in judgment on them, clearly preferring to leave the work of judgment to God (5:12–13). His concern, by contrast, is with those in the church. Are they living to the standards that are required of them?

There is quite vividly a tension in Paul's argument. Obviously, he believes that Christians are called to live according to higher standards of behavior than is the public at large. Life under the gospel of Jesus is not a license to engage in immorality. At the same time, Christians are free in Christ, no longer subject to a law that, at once, demands one thing while forbidding something else. A careful reading of 1 Corinthians 6:12–20 makes that clear. We are free *under the gospel* to live a moral life, not bound *under the law* to live according to its precepts.

The particular verses in question in chapter 6 are numbers 9 and 10: "Fornicators, idolaters, adulterers, male prostitutes, sodomites, thieves, the greedy, drunkards, revilers, robbers—none of these will inherit the kingdom of God." These are extremely difficult verses to translate because several key words have a range of meaning in both the original Greek and in English. Which meaning in the Greek is intended, and how do we choose an English word that is narrow enough in its meaning to communicate Paul's intent? (This can be seen by reading the verses in a wide variety of English translations. Translators have experimented with all manner of English usages to get Paul's point across. None of them are fully satisfactory.)

A comprehensive discussion of the details could go on for pages, so I will attempt to hit only the main points. Two words in Greek, *malakoi* and *arsenokoitai*, have been translated, in various English texts, as "homosexuals," "sodomites," "sexual perverts," "catamites," and a list of other possibilities. (That alone suggests that we are dealing with a rather wide range of meaning in both the original text and its English translation.) *Malakoi* basically means "soft," and it is used in other places in the New Testament with no sexual connotation whatsoever in reference to "soft" clothing (Matthew 11:8, Luke 7:25). That use has led some biblical scholars to conclude that the word has no sexual content in 1 Corinthians 6:9–10, but simply indicates that some men are "soft." The problem with this interpretation, of course, is that these soft ones are not going to enter the kingdom of God. It's hard to imagine that Paul is saying that soft people won't be going to heaven. Again, the problem here is the range of meaning. We know that when we say that a person has a "soft heart," we mean something quite different than when we say that a person has a "soft head."

So, can *soft* mean something else? Indeed it can. In ancient Greek literature, *malakoi* can refer to same-sex behavior—not same-sex behavior in general, but a specific variety of behavior. *Malakoi* refers specifically to the "softness" of young boys who are being abused by older men, not at all unlike what we discovered as a possible interpretation of Romans 1:27. This is why the translators of the Jerusalem Bible translated *malakoi* as "catamites"—boys kept by men for unnatural purposes. Here again it appears that we are dealing with the sexual perversion in which young boys are the sexual objects of older men. On that basis I am quite happy to stand firmly alongside the blessed apostle Paul!

The other word here is *arsenokoitai*. In its narrowest definition, the word simply means "men who have sex with men." Like *malakoi*, however, the word has a wide range of meaning that makes its precise connotation hard to pin down. Personally, I have little doubt that it refers to same-sex behavior of some sort, but I am cautious about inferring from it a specific condemnation of *all* same-sex behavior because of the likelihood that it refers to particular perversions of same-sex behavior (older men sexually abusing young boys, for example), and not natural same-sex behavior between two persons, both of whom are homosexuals. It is instructive to remind ourselves that earlier English translations rendered *malakoi* and *arsenokoitai* as "homosexuals." After further study and investigation of the Greek text, and the context to which it was originally addressed, many translators are now suggesting that a better translation would be "sexual perverts," a concept that is in no way limited in its range of meaning only to homosexuals.

1 Timothy 1:8–10. This is the third passage of the Pauline corpus that has relevance to the questions before us. This is not the place to get into an extended discussion of the authorship of the letters to Timothy. It is important, however, to say that most biblical scholars believe that the letters are not actual letters of Paul to Timothy, but letters written by a member of Paul's inner circle some time after Paul's death. Why is this important? If these are not words of Paul's, but words of the community of faith that the apostle left behind, it is important to recognize that what we are dealing with here is the word of God *as it came to the church* in the generation after Paul's death. In other words, we are dealing with the continuing revelation of God to his church, opening the possibility for us to consider that God's word is living and dynamic, and that God may have a new word for a new generation of God's people.

As we might expect by now, in 1 Timothy, chapter 1, we have a long list of vices that are not dissimilar to those we have observed elsewhere. It is interesting to observe the shift in interpretation that has taken place. What in Romans, chapter 1 was considered contrary to *nature,* in 1 Timothy, chapter 1 is considered contrary to *sound doctrine.* Also, those vices no longer seem to come under the threat of exclusion from the kingdom of God (1 Corinthians, chapter 6), but now simply are not in conformity with the gospel as the writer of Timothy understands it. This suggests, at the least, that the faith community, a generation after Paul, was hearing things a little differently. I am not suggesting that the fundamental teaching had changed, but it does seem clear that the community of faith was hearing the teaching somewhat differently than it did a generation or so before. Sound familiar?

At this point we could get into the details of the Greek text of 1 Timothy, but my sense is that what we find there is quite in line with what we have observed elsewhere as we have looked at the details of other texts. I don't believe it's necessary to trod that same ground here.

God's Living and Dynamic Word

In this chapter I have tried to break open the biblical texts that are most often referred to as having relevance for our current discussions in the church regarding homosexuality. I do not suggest that these are definitive interpretations, nor do I expect that everyone will find them satisfying at every point. But such are the challenges of the hard work of interpreting an ancient book of texts that we hold to be sacred. These texts are a living and dynamic word through which God speaks afresh in every generation. God's people through many centuries have heard the texts differently, varied according to the needs and difficulties of the times through which they have lived, and in every case have found comfort, strength, inspiration, and direction. The times through which we are living are no different.

This may suggest to some that the word of God changes. I don't think so. *We* change. That's the bottom line. Our own journey into the mystery of Christ changes the way we hear the sacred texts along the way. At various times in our lives, we are powerfully drawn to certain biblical stories and insights, and over time we discover ourselves letting those go and coming to a fresh appreciation of other biblical material that once left us cold, uninspired, or otherwise confounded. *That is good news, indeed!* It is a testimony to the gift of Christ's risen spirit within us, calling us, changing us, molding us—in short, making us into the sons and daughters of God that we are meant to be.

At an earlier time in my life, I had a very different reading of each one of the texts that we have looked at in this chapter. In most cases I was dependent on a "plain reading" of the "obvious meaning" of an English translation. But for thirty-some years now, I have been a serious student of the Scriptures, and I no longer can live comfortably with a surface reading of those precious texts. The Bible often is hard to understand. It has many layers of meaning, some of which are not apparent immediately. It takes many years of devoted study just to scratch the surface. I have had the extraordinary privilege of teaching alongside some of the finest biblical scholars alive today. Many of my seminary teaching colleagues will forget more about the Bible than I will ever know. But all of them will be happy to tell you that even after a lifetime of scholarship and teaching, they are only beginners when it comes to mining the depths of the Holy Scriptures. As a hymn writer so eloquently put it, "The Lord has yet more light and truth to break forth from his word" (*The Hymnal 1982*, no. 629).

Several years ago, while I was teaching at the School of Theology, in Sewanee, Tennessee, we enjoyed a series of lectures by a distinguished visiting professor of biblical interpretation. The subject was "Hate in the Bible." He presented fine lectures, and we all learned a great deal about an important topic. But in the discussion after the final lecture, a man stood up and asked a question, not about hate in the Bible but about homosexuality. The way he shaped his question made it clear that he was coming from a conservative, if not fundamentalist, position on the matter. Our visiting professor answered him by saying, "Friend, you should read the Bible more." He went on to say that if you want to pick a small handful of verses and interpret them in a rather narrow way, then you can easily fortify the conclusions that lay behind your question.

After a few more exchanges on hate in the Bible, another gentleman stood up and, once again, asked about homosexuality. This time it was clear from the question that he was coming from a more progressive, if not liberal, viewpoint, and wanted some help fortifying his position. Our visiting professor answered him by saying, "Friend, you should read the Bible more." He went on to say that if you want to pick a small handful of verses and interpret them in a rather narrow way, then you easily can fortify the conclusions that lay behind your question.

I think we were all struck by the integrity and wisdom of the visiting professor's response. We all need to read and study the Bible more, not to fortify the prejudices we bring to the text, but so God's living and dynamic word can be used by the Holy Spirit to teach and convert us, over and over and over again.

The Place We Find Ourselves

IT IS NO SECRET THAT the Episcopal Church, together with other provinces of the Anglican Communion and many of our ecumenical partners, is deeply engaged in conversations, and no little controversy, around all aspects of human sexuality. These conversations have paid particular attention to the full inclusion and participation of gay and lesbian persons in the life of the church. These are not new conversations. In the Episcopal Church, we have been working and talking since at least 1973. Every General Convention from then until now has, in one way or another, dealt with the subject. In the meantime much of the legislation of diocesan bodies has likewise been concerned with human sexuality. Dioceses have repeatedly called on their congregations to engage one another in study, prayer, reflection, and conversation. It seems clear that those parishes that have had such conversations over the years are in a very different place just now than those that have not heeded the call to engage in the dialogue.

Much that is positive has come out of those conversations. We are a safer church for all our people. Those conversations have provided the context for raising everyone's consciousness about sexual misconduct of all kinds. In the same span of years, we have revised our disciplinary canons and diocesan policies to respond more appropriately to unacceptable behavior by both clergy and laypersons. We have put an enormous effort into education. All seminarians, clergy, lay professionals, and most categories of volunteers are required to have sexual-misconduct-prevention training in order to be in positions of leadership. We are now expanding those educational efforts to all levels of parish life so that everyone, not just the leadership, can be vigilant in making the church a safe place for everyone.

Those conversations have also made it possible for many of our openly gay and lesbian brothers and sisters to find a welcome among us. I can think of few parishes in which gay and lesbian persons are not taking leadership roles on the vestry, on committees, in the choir, teaching Sunday school, or leading other important ministries at the parish level. The same is true at both the diocesan and national levels of the church. (It is important to remind ourselves that we are far more than a "national" church. We have dioceses in Taiwan, Micronesia, Liberia, Colombia, Ecuador, Venezuela, Costa Rica, Dominican Republic, Haiti, Honduras, Puerto Rico, the Virgin Islands, and the Convocation of American Churches in Europe that includes Episcopal churches in five European nations.)

As the conversation has progressed, two questions have been most agonizing for the church: Is it appropriate to ordain to holy orders gay and lesbian persons? Is it appropriate to bless the union of two persons of the same sex who commit themselves to lifelong faithfulness to each other? I want to examine both of those questions together because, in my judgment, a deeper question beneath each of them is the clue to finding a helpful answer to both.

Everyone knows that the church has had gay persons in holy orders for a long time: bishops, priests, and deacons. Our acceptance of that is well established. For most of the church, Anglican or otherwise, being gay (and more recently, lesbian) is not an impediment to ordination. It never has been. The reason, of course, is that homosexual persons who are to be ordained are also to be celibate.

Through time many gay priests have made a commitment to living a celibate life. It is clear that they have been given a special charism of grace to sustain them in such an extraordinary vow. I have known many such priests. Their lives have brought honor and glory to Christ. The sacrifices they have made are an inspiration to me and to others, who have given far less. They have offered themselves unselfishly for the building up of the Body of Christ. I am grateful to God for their authenticity, holiness, and grace.

But there are other sides of the story. We also have been served by many priests who did not possess the charism of celibacy. Outwardly and visibly they were fine priests. Their skills for ministry were as finely honed as anyone's. Their parishes were strong and vital. Their people loved them and depended on them for spiritual care and pastoral support. Sadly, they were forced to live a double life, a lie if you will, and we are all the poorer for it.

I have known such priests who have been forced to express their sexuality in ways that none of us, including them, would find acceptable. They have had to sneak around, find partners in out-of-the-way places, and then deal with the guilt and shame of living in a way that broke their own hearts. Perhaps most difficult of all, they had to live with the constant anxiety of being caught, of being spotted by someone who would recognize them, of being reported to the bishop. They were fabulous, faithful priests when it came to doing the work of ministry. They were also living a lie in the darkness of the night.

There is another possibility, too. I have known priests, in some cases quite well, who are gay and who have life partners. They are the ones who knew it was wrong to sleep around and had no desire to live a lie. By contrast, they wanted to make a mature commitment. They deliberately chose to find a partner, another person with whom they could share the joys and intimacies of a Christian household. They wanted a faithful, monogamous, loving, caring, supportive, mutually satisfying relationship *with one other person.* Some such couples I know have been together for twenty, thirty, forty, and now going on fifty years. Their faith and fidelity is inspiring.

How can that be? That is the hard question for many people. How can a person in holy orders, to whom the charism of celibacy has not been given, be a wholesome example to the flock of Christ? It goes without saying that all our bishops, priests, and deacons—straight and gay—are called to be wholesome examples, just as all members of the flock are called to live devout and holy lives. It also goes without saying that from top to bottom, we are sinners one and all. I have never known any person in holy orders who did not take the commitment to be a wholesome example with utter seriousness. I have never known a priest who doesn't get up in the morning and do everything within his or her power to be faithful, to be transparent in holiness of life, and to be a wholesome model of an honorable life. But faithful priests, like bishops and deacons, like laypeople of every stripe, are also sinners saved by God's grace and mercy.

To say, however, that gay and lesbian persons in holy orders are sinners just like the rest of us, simply is not good enough. Not by far. The deeper question is whether their life is inherently immoral, and whether they are thereby unworthy to hold public office in the church. That is the more important question.

In the previous chapter, I discussed briefly each of the texts that we regularly refer to in discussions of same-sex behavior. As I indicated there, I have come to those interpretations after years of working with those texts, together with a great deal of historical information about same-sex behavior in the ancient world. I have also laid those texts against understandings of sexuality that have evolved more recently. I expect to continue learning. What is important at this point, at least for me, is to face squarely the question raised by the interpretation of the sacred texts. Put simply, the question is this: *Is all same-sex behavior immoral and indecent in all circumstances?*

If one takes as the last word the plain, literal reading of the English text of that small sampling of verses, then the answer to that question is a clear and resounding "Yes!" Frankly, I don't see a way around it.

If, however, one understands those texts to be condemning particular aberrations of same-sex behavior that were rampant in the cultures of the ancient world—same-sex behaviors that are to be understood principally as acts of violence and humiliation—then it is possible to conceive of something that the Bible never explicitly forbids: loving, faithful, monogamous, life-giving same-sex relationships.

That is the dilemma with which we are faced: two distinct interpretations of sacred texts that we all hold dear. It is not a matter of biblical authority; it is a matter of biblical interpretation. It is clear that some of us are in one place, while others of us are in the other. Most of us, I suspect, are lingering somewhere in the middle. If there is a way forward, surely it is to be found in our mutual reverence for the authority of Scripture, framed in such a way as to allow a variety of interpretations by good, thoughtful people, all of whom are trying their best to be faithful to the gospel.

In times past, followers of Jesus have faced many controversial conflicts and issues: circumcision versus noncircumcision, rich versus poor, spiritual authority versus civil authority, slavery, national identity, baptismal regeneration, women's place in the church, and women's ordination, to name just a few. Such controversies have divided the church in the past because a variety of interpretations of the Bible were in play. We survived those controversies. We came through them a stronger and more vibrant church. Why? Precisely because the majority of the church made a commitment to keep at the hard work of Scripture study, prayer, fellowship, and mission *together*. In each case we lost some people. That was tragic, sad, and unnecessary. Over time many who left have returned, and for that we rejoice. But the majority of us stayed together, and we invited the spirit of the Risen One into our lives and our parishes, in the full confidence that God would take us to the place we needed to go. God has been faithful. That's easy to see.

For many in the church, the question of whether a priest in a lifelong, committed same-sex relationship can be a wholesome example is a thing of the past. This is often the case because many in the church have experienced the ministry of such people and have realized that there is nothing to fear. We often discover that reality is not nearly as troubling as our fear of it. In fact, I can think of two priests, each with same-sex life partners, who are really quite traditional in their theology and understanding of the Scripture, in their approach to the liturgy, and in the way they go about being pastors to those who are committed to their care. Both are loved and cherished by their people, but in both cases some of their folks have mused about the assumptions they made when they called their new rector. They assumed that a gay priest with a life partner would undoubtedly be a liberal of some sort. In both parishes they have discovered that their new priest is really moderate-to-conservative—more conservative, in fact, than either of their heterosexual, married-with-family predecessors.

Some in the Episcopal Church consider the matter settled for another reason. Some years ago a presentment (formal charges under church law) was brought against a bishop of the church for ordaining to the priesthood a noncelibate gay man. It was a long and involved judicial process that took place under the spotlight of enormous media attention. In the end the bishop so charged was found not guilty of having violated the "core doctrine" of the church. It was an important decision in many ways. The fact that the church court rendered its ruling with respect to core doctrine was troubling to some because it seems to imply varying degrees of importance within the body of Christian doctrine. This was consistent, however, with the long tradition of the church, which has regularly made such distinctions. There are clearly those matters—the incarnation, cross, resurrection, and second coming of Christ, among others—that are core doctrine and are broadly accepted in the church. They are generally creedal matters that, for most of us, are well beyond dispute, except to the extent that we debate them in order to mine their depths and appropriate them more fully into our own faith and life.

There are, however, other matters of great importance, often having to do with the ethics and morality of public and private behavior, that cannot be ignored, but that are generally held to be outside the boundaries of core doctrine. Such a distinction is not intended to reduce those matters to secondary importance, but simply to affirm that many important issues that are within the framework of the church's concern are not matters of salvation. Many in the church would make just such a distinction with respect to our conversations on sexuality, homosexuality, and all the attendant issues. Those are important, and we need to spend appropriate amounts of time and energy sorting them out, but *they are not core doctrine,* and therefore our unity in Christ need not be threatened. In fact, I would argue that precisely because the present struggles are not about core doctrine, we can engage in those conversations fully and without fear, and become, through our willingness to engage Scripture and one another, a stronger, healthier, and more vigorous home for the gospel of Jesus.

At another level are those who argue that the church makes policy in two ways, just like the government: by legislation and by judicial precedent. Because we have tried a bishop for ordaining a noncelibate gay man, and found that in so doing, the bishop violated no core doctrine, then the matter is settled, they argue—unless and until the authoritative legislative body of the church, the General Convention, says otherwise, and raises its saying-so to the level of church law, not simply a "mind of the church" resolution.

Many in the church are not prepared for non-celibate priests who live openly in same-sex life partnerships. I honor and respect their position, and I accept the fact that their sense of personal integrity will not allow them to stand anywhere else, at least for the time being, and perhaps forever. We also have many parishes in which many could accept this development while others could not; for the sake of unity, those parishes will continue to look for pastoral leadership among single, celibate, or married clergy. That's as it should be. After all, the majority of our clergy will continue to be married, with 2.5 children, a Labrador retriever, and a pre-owned minivan.

My own willingness to accept openly gay and lesbian persons with life partners into holy orders has to do chiefly with two convictions that I hold dear: *being serious about the witness of Scripture* and *telling the truth in all matters.* Allow me to explore each of these further.

The Witness of Scripture

By this point I hope the reader has some sense of my reverence for and dependence on Holy Scripture. I believe that being daily engaged with Scripture is part and parcel of a faithful life. Like everyone else, I have developed over the years some interpretive principles that guide my understanding of the biblical texts. Those principles are relatively fixed, but from time to time, I sense a movement in them that I attribute to the Holy Spirit engaging my mind and heart. Principal among these is that I insist on reading the totality of Scripture (and the tradition) through the lens of the resurrection of Jesus Christ from the dead. This does not mean that every story in the Bible is ultimately about resurrection, and it is not necessary to find Jesus under every rock in the Old Testament.

What is ultimately true, however, is that Christ is risen! This means that the world is radically different from anything we can imagine within the limitations of our human experience. In the world we inhabit as mortals, dead people stay dead. We are bound by the visible and concrete. We see things only partially, as Saint Paul reminds us. The resurrection of Jesus, however, blows to smithereens the boundaries of our human experience. We are *unbound!* It is possible to see the impossible, do the impossible, be the impossible. That which was closed is open. That which was bound is free. That which was fearful claims our confidence. That which was under law is now under grace. And all because there is a dead man walking! All because a whole new way of being has come to us by the resurrection of Jesus Christ from the dead!

As I consider what that means with respect to welcoming noncelibate gay persons into holy orders, I go again to the Scriptures. Of all the things I find there, two of Saint Paul's statements animate my contemplation. In 2 Corinthians, chapter 4, Paul is writing about the nature of ministry and his own weakness in shouldering the burden of the ministry of Christ. But his weakness is a gift that points away from himself, to the power of God working within him. "We have this treasure in clay jars [earthen vessels], so that it may be made clear that this extraordinary power belongs to God and does not come from us" (verse 7). All of us who are engaged in ministry in the name of Jesus—laypersons, bishops, priests, and deacons—are cracked pots, doing what little we can, out of our own brokenness, for the glory of the Lord Jesus Christ, and we are stunningly clear about the fact that the extraordinary power we share, on this side of the resurrection, is God's alone. The mission is God's, not ours. Yet to us, no less than to the least of all the saints, is given the gift to go where God is, carrying along with us all our sin and brokenness, and for a moment of eternity, to stand at God's side.

In Galatians Saint Paul reminds the saints that they will be known by the fruits of the spirit of the risen Christ dwelling in them. We will know those who have turned away from the desires of this world and embraced the fruits of the Spirit. Their lives will model for us love, joy, peace, patience, kindness, generosity, faithfulness, gentleness, and self-control. That is the basis on which all our lives, and the ministries of those in holy orders, should be counted as worthy. Do they bear spiritual fruit worthy of the Gospel of our Lord Jesus Christ?

Telling the Truth

My second conviction has to do with *telling the truth in all matters*. I am often asked why I voted yes to the election of a priest who is an openly gay man living faithfully with a life partner to be the bishop of the Diocese of New Hampshire. Although I can cite a variety of reasons, theological and personal, in the end it was about *telling the truth*. Let me try to describe that moment in my personal journey.

As a bishop with jurisdiction, I am called on from time to time to give my consent to the election of a bishop in another diocese. I generally come to that task operating under the assumption that I will say yes. I do this for several reasons. Having been through an episcopal search process several times, I know what goes into it, at both the procedural and personal levels. Having survived an episcopal election, I know first-hand something of its burden. When a diocese elects a bishop, I believe that it does so intentionally, thoughtfully, prayerfully, and under the guidance of the Holy Spirit. Because I have lived or served in half a dozen dioceses over the years, I am aware of how distinctively different dioceses can be, and in light of that, I believe that the local diocese can best discern the sort of person they need to elect as their bishop. There is also, in our Episcopal Church polity, an inherent "diocesan rights" dimension, not dissimilar to the "states' rights" provisions of the American system of government. All these factors taken together require me to have a good reason not to consent to the election of another bishop.

In the consent process for the bishop-elect of New Hampshire, I withheld my judgment so that the canonical consent process could play out. From the day of his election, we all knew that, unlike most, this consent process would be controversial. I thought it better not to make my own decision until the matter was debated on the floor of both houses of the General Convention, and to deliberate, pray, and take counsel with my fellow bishops. Waiting until the very end of the process to come to a final decision was painful for me. For many with whom I live and work, the decision was easy—one way or the other—but I was painfully aware that they are not forced, as I am, to bear the burden of the church's unity, a primary aspect of a bishop's ministry. It was also difficult for me not to pick up the phone and call Canon Robinson, a man I have known and respected for many years, and assure him of my support, as I did with several others who were seeking consent as well. That was not fun.

As the bishops gathered in Minneapolis, it was interesting to get a sense of which way various bishops were likely to vote. Several that I would expect to vote no were firmly in the yes column. The reverse was true as well. When the votes were tallied and the results made public, there were some surprises in both directions. It was also clear that some bishops did not vote their personal convictions because of how that would be received when they got home. I suspect that was true in both directions as well.

In the House of Bishops, we discussed the matter in small groups around our conversation tables, and in open debate, with the gallery open for the entire world to see. The debate was passionate but civil. It was thoughtful and prayerful. All were fully conscious of the weight on our shoulders. Whether one agrees or disagrees with the outcome, one has to be proud of the manner in which the General Convention handled those matters. It was a quintessentially Anglican gathering. The proceedings were full of holy moments.

As the debate unfolded, I found myself increasingly vulnerable to many of the arguments of those who were urging the bishops with jurisdiction to vote against consent. A reasonable scenario for voting no was coming into focus for me. Because my natural posture in these matters is to say yes, and because I felt myself on the verge of voting no, the turmoil inside me was raging.

Then I was struck by lightning. Or at least that's the best way I know to describe it.

Toward the end of the debate, a bishop rose to speak. He is a man for whom I have developed great love and respect. He is counted among the most conservative bishops of our church. I cherish our friendship. I believe he loves and respects me, too. I trust him, and I believe that trust to be mutual. I'd happily do business with him on any day. He told the House of Bishops that he had known Canon Robinson for many years, and that he could vouch for the fact that he was a devoted servant of Christ. He also said that he agreed with many that Canon Robinson is perhaps one of the most gifted and experienced priests this church has elected to the episcopate in a long time. But in spite of his genuine and heartfelt accolades, he was going to have to decline to give his consent because Canon Robinson is a gay man with a life partner.

If he had stopped right there, I might well have been convinced. But he didn't stop. He went on to say that he wished he did not know about Canon Robinson's personal life. If Robinson's personal life were a secret, there would have been no debate, no controversy, and there would have been great rejoicing among everyone because Canon Robinson was finally where he should be, in the House of Bishops.

In that moment it became crystal clear to me that I had a moral obligation to give my consent to the election of the bishop-elect of New Hampshire. It was time to *tell the truth*.

My brother bishop effectively argued that if Canon Robinson had lied to us about who he was and about his personal commitments, then we would have no trouble making him a bishop. Those are my words, not his, but I am confident that the meaning is the same. Canon Robinson stepped up to the plate and told the truth about himself. At no point in the selection or election process were there any secrets. It was important to Canon Robinson that everything about him and his election be fully disclosed. He placed himself, his family, and his long and fruitful ministry as a priest before the judgment of the church. It was the church's decision. Though I will not speak for him, I have come to know Canon Robinson well enough to believe that, had the General Convention declined to consent to his election, he would have obediently lived with his church's decision, returned to New Hampshire, and continued to be the faithful servant that the good folks there know him to be.

For years, in this and in many of our sister churches, we have done immeasurable harm by our unwillingness to tell the truth. The catastrophic state of affairs in the Roman Catholic Church is not about the sexual misconduct of some of their clergy. It is about the hierarchy's unwillingness to tell the truth. The people of God are a tough bunch. They can handle almost anything if you tell them the truth. They may not like it, but they will deal with it, and they will respect the messenger—if you tell them the truth. The loss of trust, and the onset of mistrust, is the result of keeping secrets, sweeping unpleasantness under the rug, and failing to tell the truth. Even among those who disagree with the consent to Canon Robinson's election, there is wide agreement that it is better that we are open and truthful about these matters. Whatever pain the present moment may cause us, it is mild in comparison to the sickness and disease that will result from continuing to keep secrets and failing to tell the truth in all things.

A number of years ago, a student of mine at the seminary went home in the spring of his senior year to have his final visit with his bishop before ordination. This young chap was at the top of his class. Any faculty member would have said, "He's the best of the best." He was smart, he was skilled, he was devoted, and he had a clear and contagious relationship with Jesus. In his interview his bishop asked him if he was gay. The young man thought it probably was not a good thing to lie to his bishop, so he told him that he was. The bishop then said that as a result of his "confession," he would not be ordained. After a few moments of stunned silence, the bishop spoke again, this time with tears in his eyes. "Son, I wanted to ordain you more than I have ever wanted to ordain anyone since I've been a bishop. Why didn't you lie to me?"

I believe that if the consent to the election of the bishop of New Hampshire means nothing else, it means that those days are over. And God's church will be all the better for it, because we have determined to be a church that tells the truth, even if we don't like it, even when it's painful. Thanks be to God!

The Blessing of Unions

The question of extending the church's blessing on the union of life partners of the same sex is, at one level, not all that difficult. If one believes that the Bible, in every circumstance, condemns all forms of same-sex behavior, then it is obvious that the church cannot condone, much less bless, such relationships. If, by contrast, one can see that what the Bible is condemning is same-sex behavior of a violent and degrading sort, behavior that will never be consistent with the standards of holy love at the heart of the tradition, then it seems possible to consider commending the blessing of the union of two baptized persons of the same sex who want to live a life in accordance with the traditional values of the church.

What I hear Christians who are gay and lesbian asking for is not some sort of watered-down, second-rate, theologically compromised way of living together. Quite the contrary. I believe that all of us hold in the highest regard the traditional values of Christian marriage. I have yet to hear anyone argue against the sanctity of marriage. At the heart of that sacred relationship are the eternal values of fidelity, lifelong commitment and monogamy, holiness of life, mutual nurture, and loving support. Who disagrees with that? No one I have ever met, at least in the Episcopal Church.

A related question before us is this: *Is the marriage relationship that we know in Scripture and tradition exclusive?* Some, of course, will say that it is, that the marriage relationship is only for men and women, and that no other combination of persons can live together in that way. For those who hold that position, not much more can be said. I don't see a great deal of wiggle room in that position.

There is, however, another way of looking at it. The marriage between a man and a woman is the framework that the vast majority of persons will naturally embrace. Because roughly ninety percent of us are heterosexual, that is the way of life into which the majority will fall. It makes perfect sense, then, that Scripture and tradition would hold up this picture of marriage as the model for all of us, for the simple reason that it will be what comes naturally to most of us.

The important idea here is *model*. The sacred promises of marriage that *most of us* will make are the biblical and theological *model* for *all of us* to emulate.

That is not a new idea. For centuries Christian writers have extolled the virtues of devoted friendship, and they often have done so in reference to the *model* of Christian marriage. Those who have committed themselves to the religious life as monks and nuns often have spoken of their life together in the cloister as having many of the same attributes as the model of Christian marriage. A wide spectrum of Christians have lived together, raising families in community, and they have conceived of their common life, their Christian householding, as a way to embrace the values and virtues of the model of Christian marriage.

Is it not conceivable, then, that we can accept the possibility that two baptized Christians, who desire nothing but the freedom to live a faithful life worthy of the gospel, could establish their household together on the model of a faithful Christian marriage? Although many will continue to argue that marriage is exclusive, through the centuries other configurations of the Christian household have existed, and have received both the sanction of the church and, I believe, the blessing of God. So, why not a union between two men or two women who desire nothing less than to have their relationship held to the same high standards of love and morality that we expect from the rest of us? Our gay and lesbian brothers and sisters are asking that their lives and relationships be held accountable publicly to the high standards of traditional Christian marriage, under the gospel of Jesus.

The answer, once again, depends almost entirely on how one reads the critical texts in the Scriptures. If same-sex behavior is always corrupt in its every manifestation, then the answer is easy: we cannot bless same-sex unions. If, however, one can conceive of the possibility of a loving, holy, faithful, same-sex relationship that is *different* in its character and essence from those behaviors that Scripture clearly condemns, then such a relationship is not only possible, it is to be desired.

This may be a good point at which to ask an obvious question: Why marriage anyway? It is important to remember that before marriage was a religious practice, it was a civil institution. The authorized coupling of human beings predates both Judaism and Christianity. It is an almost universal feature of human society, quite apart from whatever religious beliefs may be prevalent in a particular time and place. In every society that I am aware of, religious rituals for coupling, and all the attendant quasireligious customs, follow well-established practices in the cultural sphere. It often comes as a surprise to many to learn that the well-worn words of the marriage vows in the Book of Common Prayer have their roots in civil contract law, not in the Bible.

With due allowances for details, it is probably worth reminding ourselves that for most of Christian history, marriages took place under the authority of the civil government, and the church's role was to ask God's blessing on the couple's intention to keep the provisions of the marriage contract. That continues to be true today. Even as priests took over the responsibility of acting on behalf of the civic authorities, presiding at the making of the marriage contract, they did so *outside* the church. Once the civil marriage had taken place, the priest, the bride and groom, and the wedding guests marched in procession to the church to ask for God's blessing on what the civil authority had done, and to begin marital bliss with a celebration of the Holy Eucharist. That's the origin of wedding processions—the movement from the civil marriage to the church's blessing. Even today, if you read carefully the marriage rite of the Prayer Book, you will discover that the church does not marry people. We ask God's blessing on what they have done: "Now that N. and N. *have given themselves to each other* by solemn vows, with the joining of hands and the giving and receiving of a ring . . ." The rite then continues with prayers, blessings, and the Holy Eucharist.

A fair reading of its history suggests that marriage is a cultural institution that grows out of the natural desire of persons to couple. For purposes of social control and the management of property, the regulation of marriage has been the role of the civil order, and that continues to be the case today. Although the clergy have eased the lines at the courthouse by being deputized as officers of the state for purposes of witnessing marriage contracts, the primary role of the church is, and always has been, *to ask God's blessing* on the good intentions of what others have already done—the couple's commitment to each other and the ratification of that commitment by civil authority.

That raises another question: What is a blessing? This is not a simple question given to brief answers. The concept of blessing in Jewish and Christian tradition is complex. The Bible seems to have multiple definitions of blessing, and through the centuries, different philosophical and theological postures have shifted our understanding of what a blessing is, and what effect, spiritual or physical, may result from a blessing. Changes with respect to our understanding of liturgical prayer, the sacraments, and the power to bless as a dimension of priesthood have also shifted our perceptions of what it means to bless a person or an object.

As a longtime student of the liturgical tradition, I am abundantly aware that to say anything about blessing in a short space, without copious qualifications and footnotes, is a perilous undertaking. I do believe, however, that a theme runs beneath the countless biblical, theological, and liturgical variations on blessing: the theme of thanksgiving. Unpacking that one word—all its varied meanings, cognates, and uses—could itself be a lifetime's work.

A seemingly simple transaction—blessing a just-married couple—is far more complicated than it may appear at first. Are we blessing God (for the couple), or are we blessing the couple (in the name of God), or is God blessing the couple (through our acts of praise, prayer, and thanksgiving)? To even begin to do justice to that rather simple question would require hundreds of hard-fought pages of analysis. There is truth in each proposition, and each possibility has had preeminence at one or another point in the history of the tradition. Under each possibility, however, is the assumption of thanksgiving, the response of grateful prayer to the action of God, whatever that action is believed to accomplish.

A teacher of mine, when asked the question, "What is a blessing?" flippantly remarked that "to bless something is to say something nice to God about it." That quip does require fairly extensive explanation, but in the end, it is not far off the mark. In fact, it is quite helpful as long as one remembers that it is a starting place, not the finish line. In one way or another, prayers of blessing are, before anything else, prayers of thanksgiving. In those prayers we might ask God to do something (supplication), and we surely are going to offer God praise (doxology), but we are going to begin by rendering to God thanksgiving, for the person or object for which we seek God's blessing.

Remembering that this is only a beginning, how does *thanksgiving* help us to understand what we might mean when we speak of *blessing?* The best way to consider this is to put it in the form of a question: "Am I willing to offer to God the sacrifice of thanksgiving for _____?" I recently went to bless a new church. All the prayers were prayers of thanksgiving and praise: for the new church, for those who had provided for it, for the new organ, for the new font, ambo, and altar. We blessed the new church by several hours of thanksgiving. When we bless bread and wine, when we bless a marriage, when we bless *anything,* we begin with *thanksgiving.*

Taking that as our cue, then, we might ask, "What are we doing when we bless a friendship; a household; two elderly, unmarried sisters who have lived together for a lifetime; or a same-sex union?" The first question to ask ourselves in formulating a response is, "Am I prepared to offer thanksgiving to God?"

Some years ago I was in London for an international meeting of Anglican liturgical scholars. During the meeting one of the bishops from New Zealand showed us a draft rite that was under consideration for the blessing of relationships. He stressed that although the rite could be used for blessing a same-sex union, its scope was much wider. The idea for such a rite did not originate out of a need for same-sex blessings. He told the story of two men, the owner of a hardware store and a barber, who had been friends for decades. Their businesses shared the same building in their small town. Every Wednesday at noon, for as long as anyone could remember, they pulled the shades, locked the doors, and went fishing. They were both faithful family men, joyfully married, and now with a gaggle of grandchildren. They were leaders in the community, wardens of the parish church, and the embodiment of all that was good and true and beautiful. The church wanted to bless their relationship; that is, the church wanted to *give thanks* for their friendship, for the icon of goodness and faithfulness that they had been for a lifetime, and to seek God's continued blessing on the loving example that they had been, for all who took the time to notice.

I tell this story not to trivialize the serious lifelong commitments that any of us, gay, lesbian, or straight, desire. Rather, I want to underscore the possibility that there may be multiple relationships between good and faithful people whose lives have been lived among us in such a way as to make us yearn to give thanks to God for them. This, I believe, should be the basis for the blessing of all relationships—marriages, same-sex unions, friendships, fellow householders, monastic communities, and lots of other variations that God's people have known through time. We should bless them, bless God for them, ask God to bless them, *because we are thankful* for their life and love, their faithfulness, their joy in the Lord, their delight in their humanity—whatever it is that becomes the source of our gratitude.

People enter into relationships with each other. There doesn't seem to be a great deal that we can do about that. Some of those relationships are good, life-giving, and holy. Some are sexual; others are not. Some are characterized by mutuality and love; others by humiliation and abuse. Some are lifelong and committed; others seem to be serial. There surely are going to be some relationships that we never are going to be grateful for, because the traditional values we desire to see will never be visible.

But what about those relationships that *are* faithful? What about those in which the traditional values of fidelity, gentleness, monogamy, mutual love and tender support, devotion to Christ, and lifelong commitment are embodied, lived, and exalted? There are relationships that I am not prepared to bless. There certainly are marriages that I have blessed that have so clearly fallen short of the high standards of the marriage covenant that I don't know whether to laugh (with contempt) or cry. And there also are other relationships I have seen—some unique households, some same-sex couples, some Christians living together in community—that I have no trouble offering up to God in praise and thanksgiving. I can thank God for them because they aspire to the high standards of love and grace that are the heart of the model of Christian marriage. I can thank God for them because the risen Christ is so visibly present that to do otherwise would be an affront to the goodness of the Lord.

"All May, None Must, Some Should"

A phrase in the Anglican tradition, a shorthand of sorts, may help us just now. It derives from debates among catholic and evangelical Anglicans of earlier times over the necessity of private confession (the sacrament of reconciliation). In trying to capture the sense and shape of the Exhortation to Confession in the early prayer books, it was said that "all may, none must, some should." Capturing a marvelous spirit of generosity, those words also capture a certain practicality at the heart of the Anglican way: We claim a certain freedom for those who need to, we protect the consciences of those who are not ready by making no requirements, and we anticipate that others will discover their own desire in God's good time.

That sort of mutual love and respect, long embedded in the Anglican consciousness, can serve us well in these days. We have never been a people that required uniformity in order to express the deeper unity that comes as a gift of the spirit of the risen Christ. It is clear that we have many parishes that are not yet prepared to welcome a noncelibate gay priest as their pastor. At the same time, other parishes are not only ready, they have already done so. Their common life and ministry has been richly blessed because God's spirit led them to the priest who has the right combination of skills, experience, holiness of life, and good humor to lead them through the next phase of their parish's development. The question is, can two such parishes live together, serve together, and do mission together beyond their local boundaries? I believe that they can. *All may, none must, some should.*

It is also clear that some of our parishes and their priests are not yet ready to bless the unions of those who live together in holy, faithful, monogamous, lifelong same-sex relationships. They are more than willing to fully welcome gay and lesbian persons into their fellowship, but they are not ready to take a step toward offering thanks to God for the gay or lesbian household in their midst. Other parishes, by contrast, have reached out, for some years now, to their gay and lesbian households, and provided for them a wide range of sacramental pastoral care for the support of their lives together. Other parishes have stopped short of such ministry because it is not yet officially sanctioned by the church, but they are ready, indeed anxious, to have a way to ritually support their gay and lesbian brothers and sisters who are willing to make the sort of high-stakes commitment to each other that is readily available to their heterosexual fellow members. The question is, can parishes that are in different places in these matters live together, serve together, and do mission together beyond their local boundaries? I believe that they can. *All may, none must, some should.*

I believe that the Episcopal Church is broad enough, deep enough, and strong enough for us to live together in commitment to the Lord of the Church, in spite of being in quite different places on these matters. Our unity need not be imperiled because of a lack of uniformity in these matters. We have been to just such places before, and because of our willingness to hold on to one another, we emerged a stronger, healthier, more faithful church. Living together in tension and disagreement is always preferable to schism. Always. Tension and disagreement will work themselves out over time. Schism is irreparable.

All may, none must, some should.

TOWARD THE FUTURE
Directions and Reflections

THIS IS AN EXCITING TIME to be the church. It is a wonderful time to be an Episcopalian. The fact that so many people are using this time to study the Scriptures more vigorously is a marvelous gift. People are talking with one another, listening to one another, and engaging one another in important dialogue. I sense these days that people also are praying—for their church, for their bishops and other clergy, and for one another—and the graceful space that prayer is providing is rich, transformative, and holy. I am firmly convinced that the church will come through these days stronger, more vigorous, and, most important, more faithful to the gospel of Jesus. I am grateful for the privilege to be a bishop during these days of the church's latest reformation.

Among the questions I am asked most often is, "Where do we go from here?" In this chapter I want to reflect on that question through three lenses: midrash, orthodoxy, and pragmatism. Through each of those lenses, I want to explore the potential of understanding and authentic Christian discipleship, not as a matter of fixed belief, but as the center of dynamic faith. In our increasingly polarized world—rich or poor, capitalist or socialist, conservative or liberal, northern hemisphere or southern hemisphere, east or west—we are losing any sense of the *via media*, the middle way, the middle ground, even the middle class, socially, politically, and economically. The ideological extremes get all the media attention and most of the money. Walking courageously down the center, embracing the best of both sides and holding at bay the dark dimensions of the extremes, seems to be a diminishing option. The spirit of the times appears to be calling us to abandon the middle and to make a mad dash for polar positions.

This state of affairs, of course, is not new. At hundreds of times in church history, not to mention world history, people have separated themselves according to opposing viewpoints. The strong center, which embraced the truth from each end of the spectrum, seemed for a time to be unable to hold, powerless to maintain the creative tension that binds diverse perspectives together. The English Reformation is a good example. From early in the sixteenth century to deep into the Elizabethan settlement, toward the century's end, the pendulum kept swinging widely between polar positions: between foreign papal control and sovereign control by an adulterous monarch; between the rigidity of medieval Catholicism and the strict reforms of continental Protestantism of a Calvinist bent; between Scripture alone and tradition alone—the list could go on and on. Those were maddening times as the pendulum cut its path from one extreme to the other. Eventually, however, the pendulum's swing was more controlled, its time-keeping movement more moderate, its range of motion hovering near a more gracious center. My sense of the present days is that the pendulum is in full swing; how many times it will rush past the middle of its course is unknown. I have full confidence, however, that in God's good time, the great pendulum of our life together will once again hover near that gentle center around which the best of all of us—and the richest truth to be told—will be found holding strong.

Scripture—Midrash

At earlier points in this conversation, I have made a variety of suggestions with respect to the interpretation of Holy Scripture. Many other approaches might have been considered as well. As we look to the future, however, I believe that considering a midrashic approach to interpreting the Scriptures will help us work our way through the present conversations and provide a rich context through which the spirit of the risen Christ can instruct us and animate our witness.

A midrashic approach to Scripture might be thought of as a process of discovery. In the Jewish tradition, the texts of the Hebrew Scriptures have not been thought of as static documents to be interpreted in a singular way for all time. Quite the contrary. The sacred texts are a vital part of the life of the community of faith. The interpretation of the texts is a dynamic process in which various interpreters engaged the texts, actively sought the interpretation of others, and tracked down the insights of the rabbis who had gone before them. Out of the richness of this multivoiced conversation, faithful readings of the holy texts emerged in response to the questions and concerns of a particular time and place.

The process of midrashic discovery is not a closed system. The Talmud, for example, is an honored collection of midrashic interpretations that began to be developed several centuries before the birth of Jesus, and was completed several centuries afterward. To this day biblical interpreters consider the Talmud to be a valuable resource for understanding the variety of opinions held by the rabbis, over several centuries, on the interpretation of the Hebrew Scriptures. The Talmud, however, does not close the door on further conversation. By its very existence, the Talmud encourages the continuing process of dynamic interpretation. It is simply one important collection of voices to add to the conversation. The work of interpretation moves forward precisely because we are dealing with a living word.

The New Testament as a whole possesses many of the qualities of midrash. Rabbi Jesus, for example, brings into play new interpretations of the Hebrew Scriptures, many of which were radically different from what previously had been taught. Saint Paul, at a variety of points, enters into dialogue with the received interpretation and emerges with new insights, many of which counter the prevailing wisdom. Saint Luke, in the Acts of the Apostles, helps us to see the struggles of the ancient church caught between the widespread interpretation of the Hebrew Scriptures and what it means to be the people of a new covenant called together by Jesus Christ. The whole of the New Testament can be seen as the story of the ancient community of faith trying to discover what it means to honor their inheritance while at the same time venturing to figure out what it means to live in response to the resurrection of Jesus Christ from the dead. It is not surprising that in the living, dynamic community of faith in the New Testament, we find different interpretations, different perspectives, and different ways of knowing what it means to live in the power of the resurrection. In fact, the New Testament does not present one unified community of faith; in it we see many communities of faith, each searching to discover its own way to be people of faith living in response to the life-giving power of Christ's risen spirit.

The midrashic approach to working with the sacred texts also has a formative quality. I often hear people ask, "What does the Bible say about such and such?" As I read the history of biblical interpretation, I do not see much evidence that leads me to believe that a question like that was ever primary, at least not in the sense that we use it today. Of course, biblical scholars and preachers through the centuries have cared a great deal about what the sacred texts actually say. I can point to no period of interpretation in which the sacred texts themselves were not primary. The question above implies, however, that one might be inclined to jump from the biblical text to the immediacy of its present application—the point of present concern—without any intervening formation. So far as I can see, that approach to biblical interpretation is of relatively recent vintage.

A midrashic approach, by contrast, forms the mind and heart of the believer over a long period of time, so that in light of that formation, the believer can answer a slightly different question: "What *do you believe* the Bible teaches about such and such?" Answers to that question do not come from an engagement with the Scriptures that limits its concern to finding a durable answer to a specific question. That limited approach nearly always will lead to partial understanding, if not misunderstanding, of the sacred texts. In other words, it is difficult, if not impossible, to move directly from the biblical text to its present application without engaging the midrash. We enter into midrashic discovery as

- we read and study the full depth of the sacred texts
- we approach the Bible not as a collection of static texts but as a living and dynamic word
- we enter into conversations with others, of all times and places, who have also sought understanding of the sacred texts
- we listen carefully for how the spirit of the risen Christ may be speaking to us in the voices of others
- we enter into discovery in the full confidence that God is going to change us through it
- we recognize that discovery is a lifelong process that is never finished and definitive
- we stay in eucharistic fellowship with those with whom we disagree so that the work of midrash can continue

I have known something about this approach to understanding Scripture since studying the Bible in college. It was not until I lived among

Episcopalians who prayed the daily office in community at least twice a day that I began to experience its power to change me. If one attends to the Scriptures of Morning and Evening Prayer in a disciplined manner, one cannot help but find in those texts an aspect of midrashic discovery. In the course of a year, the readings from the daily office cover large portions of both the Old and New Testaments. Because the arrangement of the readings is not as sensitive to the liturgical year as the readings that are appointed for Sundays and feasts, one might hear readings about the betrayal of Jesus and his trial and crucifixion in the middle of Advent, or stories that we associate with Pentecost in the middle of Lent. It is amazing—and the richest sort of spiritual food—for such "collisions" to enter into our instruction, meditation, and discernment. On many occasions I would be working hard on the interpretation of a text in preparation for preaching, only to hear an unrelated text at daily office and discover in that text a new aspect of the conversation. It's not that the text that I heard at the office changed the way I thought about the text I was studying, but I became vividly aware that the texts at the daily office were forming and changing me. So changed, I would return to my study and re-engage the preaching text before me as a different person. Midrashic discovery works like that. We do not enter the work of biblical interpretation to change God's word, but to be changed by it. The text that changes me might not be the text before me, but some other. It is a life-long process, always done in community, always done prayerfully, always done in the full recognition that what we know now is only partial.

Midrashic discovery invites us into the constant re-engagement of the sacred texts, into a life-changing journey into their deeper meaning. If we take seriously the perspectives of those who have gone before us, we begin to see that it is the journey that is important, not the destination. This does not mean that the Scriptures are always up for grabs and that they are open to any interpretation imaginable. It does mean that we understand the Scriptures to be a living and dynamic word through which the Holy Spirit continually speaks afresh to God's people. Every new generation, then, is called to enter into a process of midrashic discovery, in order to hear what God would have them know, in their time and place, so that their lives might be filled to overflowing with the risen life of Christ. In these days we can expect no less from one another.

Reason—Orthodoxy

In the last few years, we have experienced a sudden increase in the use of the term *orthodox*. It has taken on a particularly virulent form that essentially means, "If you agree with me, you are orthodox; if you don't, you're not." To be "biblically orthodox" means that you share the views of those who hold a particular interpretation, sometimes even on matters that the Scriptures do not address. Others speak of the orthodoxy of apostolic faith and practice, implying that the church through the centuries, up until the present time, has always been of one mind and heart about all things; it speaks of the "golden age" of the ancient church, when there was perfect unity in all things. Such a time never existed.

When we speak of orthodoxy, we often do so in reference to heresy. It is interesting how in recent discourse we seem to have flip-flopped the historical meaning of those terms. In our present usage, *orthodox* appears to refer to a well-defined, rather rigid set of parameters within which the truth is to be found. Within that framework a strict sense of objectivity reigns, with little or no room for debate. Most of the energy in the system is expended on maintaining the status quo. There is no room for talking about the human experience of the holy (except to the degree that it confirms the status quo), and little allowance for the possibility that God might be doing a new thing among people of faith. The boundaries that differentiate those who are "in" and those who are "out" are articulated in black-and-white terms.

Although we are generally too civil to say so, those who are not orthodox are thought to be heretical, if not heretics. Their life of faith has somewhat more porous edges; they prefer to discover the truth in the infinite variety of ways that God is revealed to us, in Scripture and traditional doctrine for sure, but in other ways as well. This so-called heretical view is not without some sense of objective truth at the center, but it is inclined to be open to God's continuing revelation, through God's word and Holy Spirit, through the lives of the faithful, and by means of the continuing discernment of the church as the embodiment of the risen life of Christ. Debate and discovery are taken for granted. The great expectation is that God is alive and, with high delight, doing a new thing among us. The boundaries that separate the "in" from the "out" are not always clear.

Against the background of centuries of church history, it appears that we have things reversed. Classical Christian orthodoxy is not a closed system. At the heart of orthodoxy is the passionate search for truth, ultimately revealed, we believe, in the sufferings, death, resurrection, and promised second advent of Jesus Christ. This truth is so deep, so broad, so high that it cannot be contained in any particular formulation, understanding, doctrine, liturgy, or way of life. The truth is rich and multiform. It can be sought in the obvious places—Scripture, sacraments, creedal affirmation. But it is also to be found along the path of any honest pursuit of it, precisely because the search for truth always leads us to God. Orthodoxy is an open system in which divergent experiences, differing understandings, and various interpretations join hands in the pursuit of that deeper truth that we know to be union with the risen Christ. Orthodox theology holds together in tension those theological realities that we at first perceive to be contradictory: human and divine, nature and grace, good and evil, light and darkness, justice and mercy, sin and forgiveness, human depravity and God's unconquerable love, to note just a few of the possibilities. It is out of such contradictions—tensions pulsating with divine energy—that enduring faith emerges.

In the broad sweep of church history, the heretic was often the voice that had no tolerance for ambiguity, the one who believed that the truth of God had been cornered in clear and irrefutable terms. It was not that the heretic's opinion was necessarily wrong or theologically untenable, but rather that the heretic had become something of a johnny-one-note. The heretic was unwilling to allow the truth as he envisioned it to stand alongside the truth as others were discovering it, thereby making it impossible for the community to find the still deeper truth for which all were searching. The heretic was the one who could not live in the tension between, for example, works and grace, and found it necessary to pick one and reject the other. Orthodoxy expelled the heretic, not necessarily because he was wrong, but because of his unwillingness to seek the truth as a shared experience of faith within the community of Christ. The heretic operates from a position of fear. Orthodoxy operates from a position of confidence, trust, and the ultimate truth of God in Jesus Christ.

Claiming one's orthodoxy to the exclusion of another may simply be a more civil way to call another a heretic. Wisely, even in the most contentious times, the church has always been reticent to speak of another as a heretic; it has also been cautious about claiming for itself a purist form of orthodoxy. That means, I believe, that the church embraces orthodoxy as the dynamic reality of faithful believing infused with the power of God's spirit, not as a static framework of right belief against which all manner of things must be judged. Being orthodox is less a matter of believing a certain thing and more a matter of living a certain way. It is less a matter of making up my mind about a particular issue and more a matter of placing myself within the conversation. The Anglican and Episcopal traditions of Christianity are profoundly orthodox not because we possess the truth, the whole truth, and nothing but the truth. Our traditions are profoundly orthodox precisely because we are willing, in confidence, trust, and faith, to engage the conversation—any conversation—because we are fully convinced that the truth toward which all such conversations move us is nothing less than the ultimate truth of the risen Christ.

Tradition—Pragmatism

Back in chapter 1, we noted that the Episcopal tradition is pragmatic in contrast to many of our sister churches that are confessional or experiential. We are held together neither by a codified body of doctrinal agreements nor a common experience of God that is, in some way, binding on all. We are, instead, a pragmatic tradition that finds unity not in the uniformity of belief or experience but by means of a common commitment to particular ways of practicing the faith of the church. We subscribe to the practical approach of doing certain things together, in common, over and over for a lifetime, and we are thereby shaped and formed—each and every one of us, and all of us together—into responsive servants of the risen Christ. The pragmatic way is, at its heart, an invitation to live a disciplined life.

The pragmatic approach to practicing the faith of the church is captured in five actions. These actions shape our identity as the baptized, enrich and inspire our living of the baptized life, and call us, by the very doing of them, to renewed service to the whole of God's world. Although there is nothing about these actions that we would not share with all Christians, these actions are deeply rooted in the Episcopal-Anglican consciousness. The doing of these things is the glue that holds our life together.

1. We say our prayers. Of all that you might say about Episcopalians, we are a praying people. All Christians pray, of course, but the life of prayer has always been an identifying characteristic of the Anglican tradition. It is no accident that, next to Scripture, our most treasured possession is the Book of Common Prayer.

When we speak of our life of prayer, we mean, in the first instance, those prayers that we hold in common and generally pray together. The prayer that is the liturgy, whether of Holy Baptism or Holy Eucharist, is the primary prayer that shapes our lives. That prayer is enriched by the daily offices of Morning and Evening Prayer, together with the little offices of Noonday and Compline. We add to those the prayer that accompanies the feasts and fasts of the liturgical year and the further depth we experience in the church's prayer at ordinations or the consecration of churches.

Many spiritual masters have reminded us that the liturgy is the church's school of prayer, the place where we learn to pray, the ritual context that shapes our prayerful response to God. When we speak of prayer as a characteristic of Anglican life, we always mean the prayer that we hold in common. Most of the time, of course, we offer our common prayer together in our parish churches, or in other settings where we are in fellowship with one another. At other times we open the Prayer Book and offer the prayers that we hold in common in the privacy of our homes, on an airplane, or on a private retreat. Even then, in the solitariness of the experience, we are offering common prayer with our sisters and brothers of all times and places.

Our rich foundation of common prayer often motivates Episcopalians to venture into other modes of prayer and spiritual formation. Some of us claim the resources of the catholic tradition—retreats, centering prayer, spiritual direction, private confession, rosaries, icons, and devotion to the Blessed Sacrament. Others of us claim the resources of the evangelical tradition—renewal weekends, prayer and praise gatherings, free prayer, private devotions, and small-group meetings for spiritual nurture and support. Still others embrace a generous mixture of both. Those enrichments, however, are valuable parts of our life precisely because at the center of it all is a rich and powerful life of common prayer that shapes in us a foundation of faith and believing that forms the foundation of the whole of our life together.

2. We attend to the word of God in Scripture with our minds and our hearts. Hearing and preaching the Scriptures in the public assembly of the church holds a special place in the Episcopal Church. Few churches read more Scripture in their Sunday and feast-day liturgies. We have learned through the centuries that hearing the word proclaimed as we gather together for the liturgy animates the word in ways that are often quite different from the ways we hear the word when it is read silently in the solitude of personal devotion. Our preachers tend not to preach topical sermons that are the standard fare in many denominations, but rather to break open the gospel of Jesus, and other assigned texts of the day, so that the word of Scripture can point us all the more powerfully to the Word who is Jesus Christ our Lord. The public hearing and preaching of the word is an extraordinary gift.

We are also faithful students of God's word. The Bible is a complex book. It is not easy to understand at many points. The story line is hard to follow unless you have an experienced guide. Multiple voices in both the Old and New Testaments often seem to be saying quite different things, but with a little work, one can see that they are saying the same thing in different ways. At other times they really are saying something quite different, and we need to be attentive to that. To understand what the Old Testament writers are talking about, one has to have some understanding of their world, their culture, their political structures, and the way they used language. In the New Testament, the gospel writers will sometimes use the same story or teaching of Jesus to make quite different points. Understanding Saint Paul is often like coming into the middle of a conversation that has already begun. Many biblical texts are addressed to quite specific situations from which we can learn a great deal, but the application of those texts to our own time and place can be difficult, to say the least.

This doesn't mean that we just throw up our hands and quit, saying that the Bible is too hard. It also doesn't mean that we can read the texts of Scripture at a surface level, share what it means *to me*, and believe that we have done faithful Bible study. No matter how hard it is to understand the Scriptures, as faithful people we never can push them aside and act as though they do not matter. We must, instead, develop a lifelong commitment to faithful, thoughtful study of the Scriptures. We must engage our minds to the best of our abilities, and discover the unlimited treasures that await those who are willing to dig beneath the surface.

The Scriptures are too important to study casually. Reading the Bible devotionally is a good and holy thing, and the Spirit works mightily within us as we do so. But reading for personal devotion is a quite different thing from Bible *study*. As Episcopalians we have never been afraid to study the Bible, and to bring to that work every possible tool that we have available to us, to assist us in learning more about it. Some traditions, often those that espouse a high view of the Bible, have been reluctant to use the tools of modern critical scholarship to get to the depths of the texts. By contrast, Anglicans generally have not been fearful of mining the sacred texts to the fullest extent of our capabilities, knowing full well that at the end of the day we still are dealing with nothing less than the word of God. In fact, I believe that our willingness to engage the study of Scripture with every resource that we have at our disposal is actually a *more reverent* posture toward the Scriptures, specifically because we approach them without fear, knowing full well that whatever we discover there will ultimately enrich and enlighten our faith. Those who "protect" the Scriptures are often those who are afraid of them. We are blessed to be a church that is fearless and willing to do the hard work of Bible study, and that does so in confidence and trust in the word of God.

3. We receive the sacraments faithfully. Episcopalians are a sacramental people. The sacraments of the new covenant, particularly Holy Baptism and Holy Eucharist, play a central role in defining who we are. Worshiping at the Holy Eucharist—proclaiming God's word, interceding for the life of the world, pleading the eternal sacrifice in praise and thanksgiving, and receiving the risen life of Christ in Holy Communion—is near the heart of what it means to be a Christian of an Anglican sort. When we gather at God's table, we are an interesting bunch. Some of us have done this for a lifetime, and can't imagine doing, or being, otherwise. Others of us are newcomers, and we are still adjusting to what must seem like the fussiness of the Anglican way. Some of us are strong in our faith, our lives having been nurtured in this eucharistic fellowship for as long as we can remember. Others of us have grown up in nonsacramental churches, but are powerfully drawn to the altar of God for Holy Communion week after week. Some of us have faith that is not as strong as we would like it to be, but we know somehow that if we just keep coming, if we keep on placing ourselves before the altar of God, that one way or the other, all will be well. Others of us have tried pretty much everything else, and the only thing that begins to satisfy the hunger in our souls is a life-sized morsel of the risen life of Christ.

We are high church and low. We chant and sing folk songs, renaissance motets, and rock. Some of us imagine our prayers rising before God in a cloud of incense. Others of us prefer the intoxicating aroma of row upon row of Easter lilies. We are rich and poor. We are well employed and unemployed. We are highly educated and high school dropouts. We are plain old folks just trying to get by. We are young and old. We are conservative and liberal. We are male and female. We are straight and gay. We come in every color of the rainbow. And what holds us together is our willingness—and this no small conviction—to take each other by the hand and go unto the altar of God, where we will discover that the things that appear to divide us will disappear, at least for a few moments, when we stand together on an equal footing around the table of the Lord.

In the history of the church have been those who believed that eucharistic fellowship is the summit of our life together. To reach the summit, folks had to agree on all matters of doctrine and on the correct interpretation of Scripture, and be in an imposed state of love and charity with one another. Other parts of the church have held the opposite view: that eucharistic fellowship is not the destination but part of the journey. In the midst of doctrinal debate, in spite of differing views on the interpretation of Scripture, and even in moments of stress and strain, God's people went to the altar together, not because everything was perfect, but because sharing together in the risen life of Christ would bring them along, closer to the place where they needed to be. I am glad that as Episcopalians we are in this latter group!

4. We enjoy the fellowship of the faithful. Christian life is lived together. Living in the fullness of the baptized life means enjoying fellowship with one another, not just for fun, but because it is a serious part of who we are.

I have always found it interesting that some Christians seem embarrassed about doing things together for the sheer joy of being together. We worry if the youth group has too many social functions and if it doesn't have enough programs or do enough outreach. We complain about our foyer groups because all they do is get together for a meal and an evening of conversation. The Thursday morning quilting circle is basically just "stitch and bitch," and at the rate they're going, that quilt for the homeless shelter is never going to be finished. I don't have much doubt that the young people need a good balance to their activities, and that the sacred stitchery group probably does need to pick up the pace. But the fellowship of the faithful is not simply the residual of getting other things accomplished. It is a good thing in and of itself.

It is not just a matter of having more parties, although we Episcopalians do that quite well. It is a matter of claiming the fact that we walk this way together. It is about being in conversation with one another. It is about participating in one another's lives. It is about knowing one another well enough to be able to reach out in difficult times with love and care. As human beings the majority of us are wired for community; we need to be together, we want to be together, we depend on being together to stay healthy and whole. When we are baptized, the stakes are raised even higher. Baptism inserts us into a new community of a new covenant. The saving action of God in Jesus Christ is not for ourselves alone, but for the community of grace in which we all take our place. Sharing the baptized life in community is part of the very definition of who we are.

Sharing the fellowship of the faithful therefore is not a fringe benefit, not icing on the cake, not an added "little something extra." Being together for the sheer joy of doing so is a vital part of what it means to be faithful. Whether it is part of an official function at the parish church, or simply friends having a dinner party together on a Friday evening, it is an element of the fellowship of the faithful. Perhaps it is lunch with a coworker, a joint vacation with another family, a men's retreat at the hunting lodge, or the triennial meeting of the Episcopal Church Women. Whatever its form, its time, or its place, the fellowship of the faithful is not frivolous, but essential to life together in Christ.

5. **We roll up our sleeves and serve others in the name of Jesus.** Few will question the fact that serving others in the name of Jesus is central to what it means to live a faithful life. There is an incarnational quality to Christian mission that demands of us real flesh-and-blood responses to the needs of God's world. We pray, of course, for the needs of the whole world, and we intercede in quite specific ways for those concerns and conditions of the human family that weigh heavily on our hearts. We send our money to places far and near to help relieve the suffering of others. We encourage our political leaders to do those things that are just, right, and merciful. All of those are good things, and we must continue in those ways to do what we can.

There is also a hands-on aspect of serving in the name of Jesus that is much closer to home. In the history of the Episcopal Church, we have a long-standing tradition of being a people who are willing to roll up our sleeves—to get our hands dirty—in offering specific help to specific people. It may be something that we do together as a parish or a diocese—build a house with Habitat for Humanity, operate a soup kitchen or a clothes closet, or take a medical mission trip to another part of the world. Those are good things.

It also might take the form of something much simpler. It might mean something uncomplicated like volunteering to rock abandoned babies at the nursery of the children's hospital. It could mean teaching a child to read or helping someone with homework. It might mean grocery shopping for an elderly neighbor or collecting some extra money so an inner-city child can go to summer camp. It might mean being the pen pal of a person who is in prison or spending afternoons with a dying person in hospice. Whatever form it takes, rolling up one's sleeves and doing something good for someone else in the name of Jesus is an indispensable part of what it means to be a Christian the Episcopal way.

Those five things—prayer, Scripture, sacraments, fellowship, and service—are the core of pragmatic Episcopal life. Doing those actions transcends our need to agree with one another in all things. We discover, in the doing of those things, a disciplined way of Christian living that is constantly forming in us new dimensions of the love of God. Our faithfulness in doing them together will, over time, lead us to that new place of grace and mercy, the place that, in the present moment, we cannot even begin to imagine.

I do not believe that there is any magic to being a Christian according to the Episcopal way. It is not about believing exactly what everyone else believes. It is not about having experiences of God's holy love other than those experiences that are your own. It is about practicing the faith of the church, day in and day out for a lifetime, and trusting that in the living of it, God is molding and making us into the people, into the church, that we are called to be. We are this far by grace. And grace will lead us home.

Made in the USA
San Bernardino, CA
01 July 2019